Contents

Foreword

Rob Roy MacGregor was always at home in the countryside of Scotland – a superb outdoorsman as well as an educated and intelligent man. Circumstances and ill fortune made him Scotland's most famous outlaw. His property was seized and his very surname proscribed for 40 years after his death. It is fitting that, over three centuries after his birth, a new Scottish long-distance walk was named in his honour.

An expert at moving quickly over rough country, Rob Roy also proved to be a master of the art of escape. Despite being hunted down and arrested many times, he lived to the ripe old age of 63 and died peacefully in his bed. He was buried in the graveyard at Balquhidder, where the gravestone's legend is 'MacGregor despite them'.

The route passes through many places where Rob Roy and his clansmen were active, especially around Aberfoyle and Killin. The route is steeped in clan history, Jacobite legends and tales of the Highlanders' resistance to government from London. The Way also features some interesting railway heritage and the Victorian Loch Katrine water scheme. This was the greatest achievement of municipal Scotland: it wiped out cholera overnight.

The Rob Roy Way has much to offer people from Scotland and abroad. It has been developed by enthusiasts making use of existing resources, without external funding or support. Although not an official route*, this initiative demonstrates that long walks such as this can arise from the grass roots. Rob Roy MacGregor would have approved.

The Rt Hon Sir David Steel (Lord Steel of Aikwood), 2002

* *Ten years later, the route was recognised as one of Scotland's Great Trails.*

The graveyard at Balquhidder where Rob Roy is buried: see page 15

1 Planning to follow the Way

The Rob Roy Way goes through many places strongly linked with Rob Roy
MacGregor, Scotland's legendary outlaw: see page 13. In addition to its historic
paths, railway heritage and glorious scenery, the Way is also rich in wildlife.
And of great importance to hungry and thirsty trail users, it links villages with
friendly hosts and historic pubs.

You don't need to be an experienced long-distance walker or cyclist to
complete this route. It is easier than the West Highland Way, for example, being
17 miles (27 km) shorter, less exposed and mainly on good terrain. It has been
waymarked, but in a few places navigation can be tricky and in poor visibility
you may need to use a compass. Nearly 20% of its 79 miles (128 km) involves
roads. Although the roads are minor, if you dislike tarmac, consider choosing
another route or using transport to avoid the 8-mile (13-km) road stretch on
South Loch Tay (Ardeonaig to Acharn).

Nobody should undertake the Rob Roy Way casually, because the weather in
Scotland is so unpredictable. On any given day, you may experience weather
typical of any season, and perhaps of all four. This adds variety, but also makes
it important to have the right gear.

This book has been written for people following the recommended direction,
from Drymen* to Pitlochry. The prevailing wind in Scotland is from the
south-west, so you are more likely to have the wind at your back, and there
may be less rain as you move north-east. Also, the more challenging parts are
around Loch Tay, by which time you'll be well into your stride. If you decide to
travel southbound regardless, note various warnings about where turnings
would be easy to miss.   *For a pronunciation guide, see page 79*

Walk or cycle?

Your first decision is whether to walk or cycle. The Way was originally designed
for walkers, but cycling, including on e-bikes, has become extremely popular.
The Scottish Outdoor Access Code asserts that cyclists (and horse-riders) are
entitled to use the trail provided that they do so responsibly. What this means
in practice is explained by a leaflet *Do the Ride Thing* which states that cyclists
should be ready to give way to walkers and horse riders, give polite early
warning to other trail users and avoid damage to soft surfaces by riding on
them, especially during and after wet weather. Much of the Way follows Cycle
Route 7 (NCN7 hereafter) and with some route adjustments, cyclists of all kinds
can complete a very enjoyable route through wonderful scenery without
damage to the trail or conflict with walkers. If you stick to the main Way
throughout, there will be places where you need to dismount and push.

Route options

Your main route decision is whether to stick to the main Way which runs for 79·3 miles (128 km) or whether to follow the detour through Glen Almond and Glen Quaich described in section 3·8. This adds 17 miles (27 km) to the distance overall, and for many walkers will be a step too far, adding at least one extra day and probably two. It leaves the Way at Ardtalnaig and rejoins it at the top of the Birks of Aberfeldy. At 30·4 miles/48·9 km it is too far to walk in a single day, but may be feasible for cyclists with suitable bikes and a willingess to carry in places. Note that since the hotel at Amulree closed, walkers need transport to split this over two days unless accommodation and food can be found. However it visits two lovely glens and a remote loch, cutting out a stretch of the South Loch Tay road. For some, it may be the highlight of the holiday and we recommend you to read pages 70 to 77 before deciding.

Another extension would be to begin from Milngavie (reached from Glasgow by train) and follow the waymarked West Highland Way as far as Drymen or Old Drymen Road, joining the Way at mile 3·9.

There are several places on the route where many or most cyclists will prefer to stick to smoother surfaces rather than try to follow the walking route over narrow sections with soft surfaces where you would have to dismount and push or carry. These are pointed out in the text and highlighted with a marginal mark. For example from Strathyre to Kingshouse cyclists may prefer to stay on the minor road that goes through Balquhidder and see Rob Roy's grave: see page 15.

A minor option is whether to follow the route into Callander. Bypassing it saves 2·6 miles and enables fit walkers who are short of time to hike the 16·4 miles (26·4 km) from Aberfoyle to Strathyre in a long second day: see pages 36-44. These are the easiest two sections to combine, because of the terrain and the shortcut.

Gradients, terrain and pace

Much of the Way follows cycleway and forest roads, but with a wide range of surfaces from smooth tarmac to rough, rocky and deeply rutted tracks. In places there are narrow paths which may be stony or muddy, and occasionally the Way follows a faint or invisible trod path through dense vegetation or moorland.

The Way provides some superb views without the challenge of extreme gradients. In the first three sections, you never rise above 220 m (720 ft) and only in 3·5 does the way go quite high, to 565 m/1850 ft (south-east of Creag Gharbh) with glorious views from this summit: see page 23. The profile below shows how the sections compare overall.

Walkers are likely to spread the walk over five to eight days, depending on their route choice, time available and the pace that they find comfortable. Table 1a (left columns) shows distances and overnights for the recommended 7-day walking

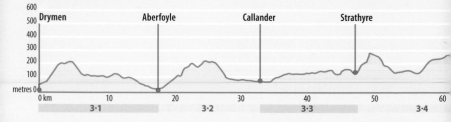

schedule as described in sections 3·1 to 3·7. For the six-day option, bypass Callander as explained above. If you have only five days to spare, the simplest solution would be to start at Aberfoyle instead of Drymen. You can create other variations for yourself, e.g. by overnighting in Lochearnhead and bypassing Killin, as explained on pages 47 and 48. Many other ways of splitting the distance are possible if you have access to any transport, or intend to wild camp, but we propose options that work for the unsupported walker who wants to stay at B&Bs and travel light.

Cyclists vary widely in their comfortable daily distances. This depends not only on the rider's fitness and experience, but also on the bike. Is its range of gears suitable to some steep gradients, are its tyres good for offroad traction, is it too heavy to lift over the occasional obstacle such as a stile – and is it electric? We propose a 4-day option that allows a gentler pace, and a more strenuous 3-day itinerary which is 3 miles shorter because it bypasses Callander. There are many other options and some cyclists will squeeze the Way into two days or even less.

Table 1a walkers' itineraries over 7 or 6 days

	7-day		6-day	
	miles	*km*	*miles*	*km*
Drymen				
	10·8	17·4	10·8	17·4
Aberfoyle				
	9·9	15·9		
Callander			16·4*	26·4*
	9·2	14·8		
Strathyre				
	13·6	21·9	13·6	21·9
Killin				
	11·9	19·2	11·9	19·2
Ardtalnaig				
	14·6	23·5	14·6	23·5
Aberfeldy				
	9·4	15·1	9·4	15·1
Pitlochry				
Total	79·3	127·7	76·7	123·4

* *bypassing Callander saves 2·6 miles / 4·2 km*

Table 1b cyclists' itineraries over 4 or 3 days

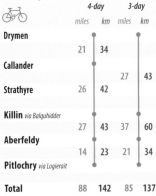

	4-day		3-day	
	miles	*km*	*miles*	*km*
Drymen				
	21	34		
Callander			27	43
Strathyre	26	42		
Killin *via Balquhidder*				
	27	43	37	60
Aberfeldy				
	14	23	21	34
Pitlochry *via Logierait*				
Total	88	142	85	137

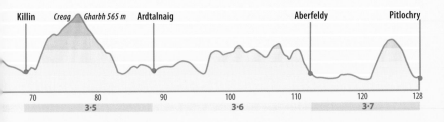

Killin   Creag Gharbh 565 m   Ardtalnaig   Aberfeldy   Pitlochry

70   80   90   100   110   120   128

3·5   3·6   3·7

Whatever you do, don't underestimate the time needed. If you're under pressure, you won't have time to linger over a glorious view, consider an interesting side-trip or simply be still enough to spot wildlife. The scenery is especially grand above Loch Tay, with the summit of the Way reached between Killin and Ardtalnaig. Consider allowing further time for side-trips up hills or mountains, from Ben Ledi to the higher mountains of the north: see pages 22-23.

What is the best time of year?

Fortunately for those who have little choice, there is no bad time of year to follow the Way. You should be prepared for cold, wet and windy weather at any time. This book was researched and photographed mainly in winter, and revisited in all seasons. If you can set off with the benefit of a recent weather forecast, winter may reward you with gin-clear visibility and more of a wilderness experience.

Here are some factors to think about:

- Winter days are less flexible, because of the short hours of daylight: at this latitude they vary from 6-7 hours in late December to 17-18 in late June.
- Winter restricts your choice of visitor attractions, open mainly from April to October.
- Winter hikers are free from insect pests such as midges (small biting insects), clegs (horseflies) and ticks (bloodsuckers that can cause Lyme disease): see page 79.
- On winter timetables, public transport is less frequent.
- In summer, more tourists are around and there is pressure on accommodation; however, from October to March many B&Bs are closed for the season.

On balance, the ideal months are probably May/June and September/October. July and August are the busiest times both for tourists and midges. Having said that, many parts of the Way are peaceful and rich in wildlife year-round. Take precautions if travelling alone, especially on exposed sections: see page 23.

Accommodation and refreshments

Suggested overnight stops reflect where accommodation and food are available. Accommodation can be scarce year-round, so book well in advance (unless wild camping). Table 2 lists the main places where you may find overnight accommodation, ranging from up-market hotels to simple, basic hostels.

If booking for yourself, tackle the most difficult location first: larger places such as Callander and Pitlochry have a wide choice so it's easy to complete the itinerary. Try checking *airbnb.co.uk* as well. Alternatively, use the specialist services of one of the expert tour operators who support the Way: see page 78. They normally offer baggage handling, book your accommodation and any transfers, and may also offer backup services in case of emergencies.

Table 2: Facilities along the Way

These facilities existed when we went to press in 2021; check before relying on them.

	B&B / hotel	hostel	pub / café	food shop
Drymen			✓	✓
Aberfoyle	✓		✓	✓
Callander	✓	✓	✓	✓
Strathyre	✓	✓	✓	
A84	✓			
Balquhidder	✓		✓	
Lochearnhead	✓			✓
Killin	✓		✓	✓
Ardeonaig	✓			
Kindrochit	✓			
Ardtalnaig	✓			
Kenmore	✓		✓	
Aberfeldy	✓		✓	✓
Grandtully	✓		✓	✓
Pitlochry	✓	✓	✓	✓

As of 2021, we knew of only two options for accommodation near Ardtalnaig, neither of which could offer an evening meal. Contact emails are given on page 78, along with details of low-cost options for Callander, Strathyre and Pitlochry. The photo shows a two-bed pod with shower and basic kitchen facilities.

The Glen Quaich option involves a logistic challenge: unless and until the former hotel at Amulree reopens there is nowhere to stay nor find food except the Farmhouse at Corrymuck-loch. See page 70 for a possible compromise, and check online for updates: see imprint page.

Pod in garden of Holly Cottage, Ardtalnaig

Navigation, waymarking and previous experience

The origin of the Way is explained on page 78. Although you will sometimes see waymarking with the RRW logo, there are still places where you need to follow signage that may refer only to a footpath or to NCN7 rather than the Rob Roy Way. If you follow our directions and mapping closely you may have little difficulty, but bear in mind that waymarkers can become disturbed or removed by animals or humans, that vegetation often obscures them in summer and there are many different styles of waymarker to stay alert for: see photos below. Always try to keep track of your position in relation to the mapping in this book.

If you are inexperienced at long-distance routes, the Way may be suitable as your first outing, but ideally aim to go with somebody who has previous experience. Be sure to plan within your capabilities and please obtain our *Notes for novices*: see page 78.

Planning your travel

To plan your travel, consult a suitable map together with this table. There is a good train service between Pitlochry and Glasgow or Edinburgh.

Table 3: Distances and fastest journeys between selected places

	mile	km	train	bus	car
Glasgow / Pitlochry	80	129	1h 40m	2h	1h 45m
Edinburgh / Pitlochry	75	121	1h 45m	2h 15m	1h 45m
Glasgow / Edinburgh	48	77	50m	1h 20m	1h
Glasgow / Drymen	18	29			45m
Glasgow / Aberfoyle	26	42		2h 30m	1h

There is no bus service between Glasgow and Drymen, but frequent trains run to Balloch from Queen Street. From Balloch to Drymen is about 8 miles: take a taxi or a 309 bus which runs almost hourly on weekdays, a bit less frequent at weekends: *www.garelochheadcoaches.co.uk*.

To reach Aberfoyle from Glasgow use FirstBus X10A service; in 2021, five buses a day ran daily on weekdays, fewer at weekends: *www.firstgroup.com*. To reach the start and return from your finish, you may need an extra overnight in or near Glasgow, Edinburgh or Pitlochry. Glasgow and Edinburgh are well-served by rail, road and air from elsewhere in the UK: see page 78. Glasgow Airport is about 15 miles west of the city.

Public transport is ideal for the unsupported trail user. If your group has a support driver, it's easy enough to meet walkers and cyclists at a road, but please be very considerate about where you park. It is a major annoyance to landowners, and can cause real hazards, if cars or vans obstruct passing-places or gates.

Table 3 above shows the fastest scheduled times for bus and train (as of 2021). Car journeys are the best times likely within speed limits, not allowing for traffic hold-ups or any other stops. All figures are rough guidelines only: check timetables carefully before making plans. Not all services are daily and winter timetables are often restricted.

Toilets and phones

Public toilets (rest rooms, WCs) are becoming very rare in parts of Scotland, mainly because of the costs of maintenance. Instead councils often agree a 'comfort partnership' with a local business which then allows the general public to use toilets inside their buildings, free of charge: look for such signs. Public phone boxes have largely been removed or repurposed as defibrillators or self-service book libraries because maintaining them is no longer economic.

West over Loch Lubnaig

Scottish Outdoor Access Code and dogs

Scotland has enlightened laws that allow everybody access to open land, including privately owned, provided only that they exercise that access responsibly. The nature of those responsibilities is summarised above and explained in detail online in the Code.

Any long-distance route relies on goodwill from landowners, and a single careless trail user (e.g. one who leaves a gate open or fails to control a dog) will damage good relations as well as breaching the Code. Remember that the countryside provides a livelihood for its residents: your playground is their

Enjoy Scotland's outdoors responsibly

- take responsibility for your own actions
- respect the interests of other people
- care for the environment

KNOW THE CODE BEFORE YOU GO
outdooraccess-scotland.scot

workplace. Do not climb over fences or gates if there is a stile or any means of opening and re-fastening the gate. Take your litter away with you, and guard against all risk of fire. Help to safeguard water supplies and take care of wildlife, plants and trees.

Nearly half of the Way that runs offroad is on tracks owned by the Forestry and Land Scotland (FLS). During felling operations, it sometimes posts diversions and may have to close a section: always follow local signage. Be alert for timber traffic, especially on weekdays.

Take extra care around livestock. Stay well away from young lambs and their mothers, and never disturb pregnant ewes. Give cattle a wide berth, especially if they are with young. Read page 12 carefully before taking a dog along the Way.

Deer stalking is an important part of the rural economy for some estates. Deer can become victims of uncontrolled population growth, leading to loss of habitat and death by starvation. Trail users should never disrupt deer stalking on the estates that they pass through. For roe deer stalking, the season is year-round and the times to avoid are early morning and late evening. For red deer, the main season for stags is August to 20 October, any day except Sunday, and at any time of day.

The Way is generally suitable for well-behaved dogs. If you are concerned about taking your dog among livestock on Brae Farm (see page 54) you could use the South Loch Tay road instead.

Always think carefully, before deciding to bring your pet along. Dogs must be kept under close control, not only to avoid stress to livestock but also for their own safety. Do not let even a well-trained dog off the lead anywhere near livestock, especially around lambing time (March to June). A farmer who sees a dog running free near his animals will put concern for his livestock first.

If you are walking with your dog on the lead, keep well away from cattle: both dog and owner can be put in danger by this combination. Cattle protect their young fiercely, and may attack walkers, especially those with dogs.

Serious injuries and even deaths have been caused by ignorance of the danger of coming between a cow and its calf.

Finally, here are four practical points about taking your dog along:

1 If your dog fouls the path at any time, clear up after it.
2 Some sections of the Way still have ladder stiles. Lifting your dog over can be both strenuous and awkward, depending on the dog's weight and attitude.
3 Many accommodations do not accept dogs: check carefully before booking.
4 Dogs may disturb ground-nesting birds or young mammals: keep your dog under very close control during the breeding season (April to June).

What to take with you

The packing list below is intended for walkers; cyclists will have different needs, especially for footwear and perhaps panniers. Trail users should consider whether they need help with baggage-handling: see *www.robroyway.com*. If you're new to long-distance routes, consult our *Notes for novices*: see page 78. Well in advance of setting off, complete a few long hikes or bike rides, to test your gear, comfort and fitness

Packing checklist

The checklist refers to your daytime needs only, and is divided into essential and desirable. Experienced walkers may disagree about these categories, but the list is meant only as a starting-point. Normally you will be wearing the first few items and carrying the rest in your rucksack.

If you're camping, you need much more gear, e.g. tent, groundsheet, sleeping mat and sleeping bag. You'll also want a camping stove, cooking utensils and food. To carry everything on your back, you need to be strong, experienced and organised.

Essential

- comfortable, waterproof walking boots and specialist socks
- breathable clothing, including full waterproofs
- hat and gloves
- water carrier and plenty of water (or purification tablets)
- enough food to last between supply points
- guidebook, compass and maps: see p79
- blister treatment and first aid kit
- insect repellent: in summer months, expect midges, ticks and clegs– especially in still weather
- waterproof rucksack cover and/or liner, e.g. bin (garbage) bag which has many uses
- some cash in pounds sterling
- Credit and debit cards are widely acceptable and contactless payment is usually preferred, but sometimes machines are faulty or networks fail, so always carry some cash as backup.

Desirable

- compass, whistle and torch: essential if you are doing any 'serious' side-trips or hiking in winter
- pole(s)
- binoculars: for navigation and spotting wildlife
- camera, ideally light and rugged; take spare batteries and memory cards
- pouch or secure pockets: to keep small items handy but safe
- gaiters, to keep mud and water away from boots and trousers
- toilet tissue (biodegradable)
- sun and wind protection for skin and eyes
- spare socks: changing socks at lunchtime can relieve damp feet
- spare shoes (e.g. trainers or clogs)
- notebook and pen.

Mobile phone: handy for arrangements but don't rely on one for personal safety. Network coverage is patchy along the Way.

2·1 Rob Roy and the Jacobites

Rob Roy MacGregor, the third son of Donald Glas MacGregor of Glengyle and Margaret Campbell, was born in Glengyle, on Loch Katrine-side, in 1671. He spent much of his life in the Trossachs, the area of lochs and rugged hills lying east of Loch Lomond. From Aberfoyle to Killin, the Way skirts the eastern edge of the Trossachs.

Rob Roy was a man of property and was involved in large-scale cattle droving and dealing. He and his brother Iain developed the Lennox Watch, a body that offered 'protection' to cattle owners in return for money. When protection money was not paid, cattle tended mysteriously to 'disappear'. Activities like this by the MacGregors and some other clans gave us the word 'blackmail', black for nefarious deeds and the colour of most of the cattle of past times; mail from Scots and Gaelic words for rent or payment. (The larger, and mainly red-brown Highland cows that we see today are a 19th century cross-breed.)

After his father was captured and imprisoned, at the age of only 30 Rob Roy effectively became the Chief of a leading section of his pugnacious and persecuted clan. In those days the powerful Duke of Montrose was his patron.

His luck changed and his business collapsed when his drover Duncan MacDonald disappeared, taking with him the enormous sum of £1000 intended for cattle purchase. In 1712 the Duke of Montrose (to whom he owed money) turned against him and had him bankrupted and outlawed. His wife and family were evicted, and several of his houses were burned or ransacked.

Rob Roy swore vengeance, and took to the hills in a long campaign of thieving cattle, occasionally kidnapping Montrose's servants and swiping his enemies. His frequent escapes, popularity with local people and generosity to the poor all gained him a reputation as a Scottish Robin Hood. Unlike the legendary Robin, Rob Roy's life is well-documented and factual: see page 79 for some sources.

In all, he and his family lived in seven houses; two on Loch Katrine-side, two in Balquhidder and one each in Glen Dochart, Glen Shira (in Argyll) and on Loch Lomond-side. Most were ransacked or burned on occasion, and in addition he used a network of caves and hidey-holes.

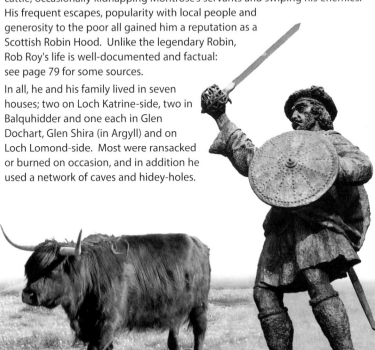

Chronology

1671	Rob Roy MacGregor was born in Glengyle on Loch Katrine-side
1689	Battle of Killicrankie was won by the Jacobites. Rob Roy and his father fought on the successful side in the first campaign of the Jacobite cause. The MacGregor surname was proscribed by William of Orange.
1693	Rob Roy married his cousin, Mary MacGregor of Comer.
1702	William of Orange died; Anne succeeded as Queen.
1707	Union of Scottish and English Parliaments took place.
1712	Rob Roy was made bankrupt by the Duke of Montrose after his drover absconded with the funds, and Rob Roy was declared an outlaw.
1713	Montrose's men evict Rob Roy's family, and they moved to Glen Dochart. Rob Roy was sheltered in Finlarig Castle, Killin for a while.
1714	Queen Anne died, and was succeeded by George I under the Act of Settlement, 1701.
1715	First Jacobite uprising ends indecisively after the Battle of Sheriffmuir, 13 November 1715.
1717	Rob Roy was captured at Balquhidder, escaped while crossing the Forth, was recaptured in Dunkeld, imprisoned in Logierait, and promptly escaped again.
1720	Rob Roy moved to Inverlochlarig in Balquhidder Glen.
1725	Rob Roy submitted to King George I via General Wade.
1730	Rob Roy converted to Catholicism at Drummond Castle.
1734	Rob Roy died at Inverlochlarig and was buried at Balquhidder.

Many stories arose from Rob Roy's fighting strength and striking appearance, with his fiery red hair: Roy comes from the Gaelic ruadh, meaning red. His air of command was backed up by impressive qualities of leadership. He was romanticised in the novels of Sir Walter Scott who claimed that Rob had unusually long arms, but there is no confirmation of that.

He mobilised most of Clan Gregor on the Jacobite side (see page 16) and he took part in the Battle of Sheriffmuir in November 1715. Later he was accused of treason because of his Jacobite activities.

The Duke of Montrose captured him at Balquhidder in 1717, but he made a daring escape while fording the River Forth en route to Stirling Castle. He was recaptured by the Duke of Atholl in Dunkeld and imprisoned in Logierait, but he escaped again after only one night. Eventually, with support from the Duke of Argyll, he received the King's pardon in 1725.

He died in his bed at Inverlochlarig nine years later, and was buried in the Kirkton of Balquhidder where his wife and two of his sons were also later interred. There was a massive attendance at his funeral. He had outwitted two dukes and the British Army, and much that was good in the life of the old Highlands went with his passing.

Rob Roy's grave, Balquhidder: its legend asserts the surname

MacGREGOR DESPITE THEM

The legend on his gravestone 'MacGregor despite them' is a defiant response to proscription – the Hanoverian Government's attempt to destroy the clan by forbidding any use of the surname MacGregor. Proscription prevented clansmen from entering into legal contracts, as happened on several occasions. The most recent prohibition was lifted in 1775.

After the clan took to the hills, they became known as Clann a' Ched (the 'Children of the Mist'). The memory of the old MacGregors lives on to this day.

The Jacobites

In 1688, James VII of Scotland (who also became James II of England after the Union of the Crowns in 1603) was deposed by popular demand, largely because he was promoting the Catholic Church. His Protestant daughter Mary was enthroned instead, along with her Dutch husband, the Protestant William of Orange.

Those who continued to support the direct Stuart line of James VII and his son James (the 'Old Pretender') became known as Jacobites: *Jacobus* is Latin for James. The unpopularity of the 1707 Treaty of Union, together with the sense of distance from decisions made in London, gave the Jacobite cause a nationalist flavour. Additionally, most Jacobites were Roman Catholics or Episcopalians, and Highland Jacobites felt that the Gaelic way of life was under threat.

During 1689-1745, contact was kept up between Scotland and the exiled Jacobite court, first in France and then in Italy. Two famous Jacobite risings took place in 1715 and 1745. The 'Fifteen' focused on the Old Pretender and effectively ended after the Battle of Sheriffmuir in 1715. The Jacobites heavily outnumbered the Government forces, but failed to win the conclusive victory that they needed.

However, Jacobite discontent continued to flourish in the Highlands. A small Rising took place in 1719 when the Jacobite clans, including Rob Roy, were joined by a contingent of Spaniards, but it fizzled out after a short battle in Glen Shiel. The next main rising, the 'Forty-five', focused on the Old Pretender's son, Charles Edward Stuart, also known as 'Bonnie Prince Charlie'.

Although warmly acclaimed on arrival in Scotland from France, his march southward into England gained so little support there that the Jacobites retreated and hoped to hold 'Fortress Scotland' until the arrival of more French aid. The Battle of Culloden in 1746 marked their final defeat. However, Bonnie Prince Charlie remained in Scotland for another five months, living in hiding and being pursued all over the Highlands and islands by the military.

In those unsettled times, Government control of the Highlands depended on good communications, intensive patrolling and key forts. A key figure in this was General George Wade (1673-1748), Commander-in-Chief of the Hanoverian army in North Britain (i.e. Scotland). During 1724-40, he and Major William Caulfeild built 240 miles of military roads and many forts and barracks in the Highlands.

Although Wade is famous for his military roads, he thought his finest achievement was the Tay bridge in Aberfeldy: see the photo on pages 14/15. It was built in 1733 to a design by William Adam. After 280 years, it still carries vehicles without any weight restriction, thanks to its superb design and construction.

Battle of Culloden, oil painting by David Morier

2·2 Other history

Loch Katrine water scheme

The Loch Katrine water scheme was a bold response to the lack of clean drinking water for the rapidly expanding city of Glasgow. In the nineteenth century, private water companies sold water to the public from horse carts, and diseases flourished. The cholera outbreaks of 1838 and 1848 resulted in many thousands of deaths.

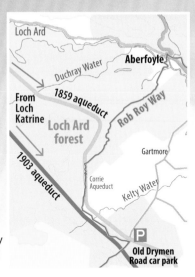

In 1853 the city fathers commissioned John Bateman, a civil engineer, to look at options for improving the water supply. He reported that the best source was Loch Katrine: there was very heavy rainfall in its catchment area and also its water was exceptionally pure.

An Act of Parliament (1855) was needed to authorise the engineering works. These were on an impressive scale:

- a huge dam to raise the level of Loch Katrine
- an aqueduct 26 miles (42 km) long to carry the water towards Glasgow
- a storage reservoir at Mugdock, just to the north of Glasgow
- 26 miles (42 km) of mains aqueduct and 46 miles (74 km) of distribution pipes to deliver the water to households throughout the city.

Astonishingly, this ambitious engineering project was completed in under four years. In October 1859 Queen Victoria opened the scheme, which was a resounding success, wiping out cholera at a stroke.

The scheme was extended by a further Act of Parliament in 1885, and a second 'new' aqueduct constructed between 1886 and 1903. Thanks to improved tunnelling techniques, this was slightly shorter than the first, with a faster flow rate. The Way closely follows the route of the 1859 aqueduct in Loch Ard forest: see diagram above.

The Corrie Aqueduct (before it was covered)

You can trace the aqueduct's route underground by spotting its rounded stone markers, as in this photo. Its most salient feature is the B-listed Corrie Aqueduct, a bridge 1000 feet (305 m) long with a single central pier. Its iron trough was technically difficult to construct, and reflected the lack of locally available stone.

You pass other impressively built structures on your way through Loch Ard forest. The stonework of the ventilation shafts speaks of Victorian pride in their design and construction: see the photo below. Walking beside the magnificent Corrie Aqueduct – completed in 1858 – you may wonder how many modern structures will still be working as well in 150 years time.

Development continued when further catchment areas were connected directly to that of Loch Katrine. Loch Arklet was completed in 1914 and Glen Finglas only in 1965. Nowadays, when full, the reservoirs hold about twelve days' water supply for the City of Glasgow and its environs. Over a million people still enjoy the legacy of this bold and enlightened scheme of Victorian engineering.

The railway heritage

From Callander to the top of Glen Ogle, the Way follows the trackbed of the Callander and Oban Line, constructed to link the fast-growing city of Glasgow with the Highland port of Oban via Dunblane, Callander and Kingshouse. Ever since Scott's novels had first made Scotland popular, romantic Victorians (including the Queen herself) were visiting in increasing numbers. The expansion of the railways encouraged this trend.

The long haul up Glen Ogle was at a gradient of 1 in 60 over an impressive viaduct built in 1870. The line was completed to Oban in 1880.

From the outset it was operated by the Caledonian Railway, which became part of the London Midland and Scottish in 1923. After nationalisation in 1948, the line continued until sadly it closed in September 1965. Doomed by the Beeching report, its closure was brought forward by a serious rock fall.

A separate branch of the Caledonian Railway had joined Perth to Crieff in 1867. This was extended westward to St Fillans in 1901 and to Lochearnhead in 1904, joining the Oban line at Balquhidder Junction in 1905. This last section was expensive to construct because of the heavy rock tunnelling and two large viaducts, one of which you see clearly from the high part of the Way when looking south towards the village of Lochearnhead.

Sadly, this line lasted less than 50 years, and after it closed in 1951 the track was removed. The Lochearnhead station buildings fell into disrepair, until the Hertfordshire Scouts (based some 400 miles to the south) saw its potential as an outdoor centre. Their bold fund-raising efforts secured its future, first by leasing it, then in 1977 they bought it. As the photo on page 20 shows, the station has been beautifully restored. If you divert from the Way into Lochearnhead (see page 47) you pass the entrance to this Scout Station and may see its platform and buildings.

> ### The stolen station clock
> Under the 1923 Act of Parliament that grouped the many small British railways into the 'big four', the Caledonian Railway fell under the London, Midland and Scottish (LMS) grouping. By mistake, the tiny Killin company was overlooked by the Act's draftsmen. The LMS behaved as if it owned it, and LMS officials removed the Killin station clock to instal it at Euston. As a result, the Killin company took legal action, and a generous settlement ensued, sparing the LMS huge embarrass-ment. The clock remained at Euston for 40 years.

Further north, the Killin Railway Company opened its line in March 1886, linking the Callander & Oban line to Killin village and its steamer service on Loch Tayside. The Marquis of Breadalbane was a major sponsor of this tiny independent company, and many local people were also persuaded to support it.

The Glen Ogle viaduct (1870)

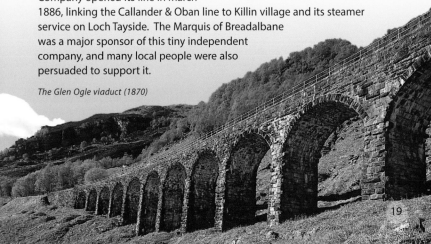

Lochearnhead station

The service was operated by the Caledonian Railway, but it was hopelessly uneconomic. Its shareholders were fortunate indeed to get their money back after the affair of the stolen clock: see panel on page 19. The Killin line finally closed in September 1965.

Prehistory around Loch Tay

In the simplest terms, prehistory since about 4500 BC can be divided into three periods:

- the Neolithic period until about 2200 BC, when the nomadic way of life gave way to farming
- the Bronze Age, from 2200 BC until about 800-600 BC, when bronze was used for making tools and weapons
- the Iron Age, when iron took over from bronze as the prime metal, from about 600 BC until the early centuries AD.

Croft Moraig stone circle, near Kenmore

The wooded shores of Loch Tay and the flatter lands of Strath Tay to its north-east have been inhabited since prehistoric times. You see many signs of this on the map and from the Way: crannogs (see below), forts, standing stones, tumuli (burial mounds) and mysterious cup and ring-marked rocks.

Kenmore is a great centre for exploring the prehistoric remains of this area. Croft Moraig is the most complete stone circle of its kind in Scotland. It stands 2½ miles (4 km) north-east of Kenmore next to the A827 on its south side (grid reference NN 797 472). Access is via a swing gate at the corner of the farm track. Although not in public care, it is in good condition and well worth a visit. Thought to be at least 4000 years old, it is more ancient than the simple four-post circle that the Way passes in Fonab Forest: see page 67.

The Scottish Crannog Centre

Crannogs are an ancient type of loch-dwelling found throughout Scotland and Ireland, occupied at any time from 3000 BC until the 17th century AD. Our ancestors built them out on the water for many reasons – as stockades for livestock, storehouses for supplies or as symbols of status and power.

Many were originally thatched round houses supported on a timber frame, based on piles driven into the loch bed. Today they are still seen as submerged stony mounds or tree-covered islands.

The Scottish Crannog Centre houses a museum of finds from crannog excavations and demonstrates ancient crafts such as woodworking, spinning and weaving, pottery, metal working and music. The reconstructed crannog in the photo below was sadly destroyed by fire in June 2021.

As a result the centre is moving to a larger site across Loch Tay at Dalerb, where that crannog will be reconstructed again, joining two other crannogs, an Iron Age village with roundhouse and perfomance and exhibition spaces. There will also be a training yard for green woodworking skills, a gift shop and café. The new centre is expected to open in 2022; for an update and visit details, see *www.crannog.co.uk*.

2·3 Munros, Corbetts and Grahams

A Munro is a Scottish mountain whose summit is over 3000 feet (914·4 m) above sea level. If seen as subsidiary to a neighbouring Munro, a 3000-foot peak is classified as a 'Top', but this distinction is subjective and can be controversial.

They are named after Hugh Munro, a London-born doctor (1856-1919). His published table (1891) listed 238 such peaks (and 538 Tops). There has been protracted debate about the total, and the exact distinction between a Munro and a Top, ever since. The Scottish Mountaineering Club's 2012 figure is 282 Munros and 227 Tops, the revised numbers reflecting more accurate survey methods.

The first 'Munroist' was the Reverend A E Robertson, who completed his final Munro (as then listed) in 1901. Since then, 'Munro-bagging' has become a popular sport. By 2018 over 6000 people had recorded their success on the SMC official list, but many more are Munroists in private.

Some determined climbers ascend all the Munros in a single expedition lasting for many months, whereas others spread the challenge over a lifetime. The average individual takes about eight years to complete his or her round.

Until recently Stephen Pyke held the record for his completion in under 39.5 days – impressive because he avoided motorised travel, using only bike, canoe and feet. Then in 2020 Donnie Campbell set a new human-powered record of only 31 days, 23 hours – an extraordinary feat of fitness, endurance, planning and mental strength.

Throughout the Way, your views are dominated by various Munros: the most southerly is Ben Lomond, whose peak you first glimpse from Loch Ard forest. Looking back down Glen Ogle, you see the twin peaks of Ben Vorlich and Stuc a' Chroin. Approaching Killin you will see the Tarmachan ridge (page 51) and along Loch Tay-side the view is dominated by the Lawers group. Ben Lawers is Perthshire's highest mountain at 1214 m/3984 feet. Beyond the northern end of Loch Tay, notice the distinctive ridge of Schiehallion (1083 m/3547 ft): see page 59. In the 18th century, experiments on this isolated, symmetrical mountain led Charles Hutton to develop the concept of contour lines.

Ben Lawers from the entrance to Fonab Forest

West over Lochan Breaclaich: see page 52

A Corbett is smaller than a Munro, with a height of 2500-2999 feet (762-914 m) and a drop of at least 500 feet all round. There are several Corbetts close to the Way, notably Ben Ledi (879 m/2875 ft) which dominates the town of Callander.

The Way passes the start of a path to Ben Ledi's summit: see map page 37 and page 42. Never underestimate this mountain: it has dangerous slopes on its eastern face and snow often lies late. Although it is partly waymarked, you need compass skills if mist descends. On a fine day, the views from its summit are excellent in all directions. There's a fine round trip, climbing from the Stank car park and, from the summit, heading on north to descend via Stank Glen. Allow about four hours for this.

Grahams are defined in metric units, with a height of 610-761 m (2001-2499 ft) and with a drop of at least 150 m (492 feet) all round. There are many Grahams near the Way, including Creag Gharbh (637 m), whose shoulder carries the highest point of the Way: see page 52.

Mountain Code

To report an accident in the mountains, telephone 999 or 112. Be ready to state your location, details of the injury/accident and your contact phone number.

Before you go

Learn to use a compass and map.
Know the weather signs and local forecast.
Plan within your abilities.
Know simple first aid and the symptoms of exposure.
Know the mountain distress signals.

When you go

Avoid going alone if possible.
Leave a note of your route, and report on your return.
Take windproofs, waterproofs and survival bag.
Take suitable map and compass, torch, water and food.
Wear suitable boots.
Keep alert all day.

In winter

(November to March)
Each person needs an ice-axe and crampons, and to know how to use them.
Learn to recognise dangerous snow slopes.
Group members may need protection, such as climbing rope and technical gear.

2·4 Habitats and wildlife

The Way runs through three main types of habitat, described below:• waterside • woodland • heath and moorland.

To improve your chances of wildlife sightings, carry binoculars and walk alone, or with others who share your interest and are willing to move quietly. Try to set off soon after sunrise, or go for a stroll in the evening. Animals are much more active at these times than in the middle of the day. Since this applies to midges too, protect your skin thoroughly, especially from May to September and in still weather.

Grey heron and chicks, nesting in tall conifer

Waterside

Much of the Way passes near water, alongside various lochs, rivers and falls. Look out for grey heron standing motionless in the shallows, hunting for fish and frogs. In flight, they trail their legs, and their huge wings beat very slowly. Watch also for signs of shy otters, such as spraints on rocks and river banks or the remains of frogs or fish.

Oystercatchers are easy to spot: look for their white-on-black M-shape in flight, and listen for their shrill piercing cries. Their long orange-red bills are good at cracking open molluscs. In winter, they congregate around estuaries, but from March to July they move inland to breed, often nesting in fields.

Oystercatcher

Near streams and rapids, look out for the dipper, a starling-sized bird with aquatic tendencies. This attractive, athletic bird often stands or wades in fast-moving rivers, plunging in fearlessly to feed on tiny fish, molluscs and tadpoles. Recognise the dipper by its shape, colour and movement, typically a fast darting flight over water.

Dipper

Woodland

The Way goes through large areas of forest, mainly productive conifers with some semi-natural woodland. The Forestry Commission Scotland (FCS) owns most of this land, and is re-structuring the conifer woodlands whilst expanding and linking the remnants of older broadleaved woodland. This involves planting native broadleaved trees, removing exotic conifers and controlling invasive rhododendrons.

Forests are also home to Britain's native red squirrel (*Sciurus vulgaris*). It is endangered by the larger grey squirrel (*Sciurus carolinensis*), an invasive species introduced in Victorian times. Greys carry squirrelpox, a disease that is fatal to their red cousins. Please report any squirrel sightings: see page 79.

Red squirrel

Wild primrose in birch woodland

In spring, the woodland floor may be carpeted with bluebells or wood sorrel, and hosts other wild flowers such as violet, celandine, primrose and wood anemone.

Woodland provides foraging ground and shelter for wildlife including foxes. The barn owl population has increased, mainly due to a long-term FCS nest box scheme in the Loch Ard Forest area, and also thanks to its woodland re-structuring. Although nocturnal, barn owls hunt in the last hour before dusk and sometimes in the early morning, particularly if they have young to feed. They prefer open woodland, farmland or moorland with plenty of long grass: see photo on page 28.

Wood anemone   *Fox in woodland*

Pine martens live in woodland

The pine marten became almost extinct in Britain and is therefore a protected species. Its rapid population rise in the southern Highlands reflects the increase in woodland. They are regularly found breeding in some of the barn owl boxes. The pine marten is the only mammal that is agile enough to catch squirrels.

Britain has only two native species of deer: red and roe, both of which originally lived in woodland. Red deer subsequently adapted to life on open upland, but their smaller cousin, the roe deer, never made the transition.

Deer are normally shy, but you may see them almost anywhere along the Way – especially if you walk alone and quietly. Once they have seen or heard you, all you'll see is kidney-shaped white patches on their fast-disappearing rumps.

Roe deer buck

Heath and moorland

Look up and you may see various birds of prey, including tawny and barn owls, which mainly depend on small mammals for their diet. Field voles live on grass, plants and fruit, and are an important part of the food chain: eight different species of bird, as well as several mammals, prey upon it. As much as 90% of the barn owl's diet consists of field voles, so it is vulnerable to any drop in this population.

Barn owl

Examples of Scots pine (*Pinus sylvestris*) are found along various parts of the Way, especially on poor soils and in exposed places, high above Loch Tay. After the Ice Age, 8000-10,000 years ago, Scots pine re-colonised Scotland, and it is the only pine tree native to Britain. Isolated trees are useful perches for birds of prey. Mature trees have a distinctive shape and strongly patterned bark.

Scots pine beside the Way at mile 76·4

Golden eagle

You have a good chance of seeing buzzard, a large bird of prey that is widespread in Scotland. They feed on small mammals, especially rodents, but will also take birds, reptiles and even large insects. Typically you will see them soaring and circling on air currents, wings held motionless in a shallow Vee, hunting for prey or carrion.

It makes a distinctive mewing call, especially in the breeding season, and sometimes perches on tree stumps or fence-posts. The buzzard is also known as 'the tourist's eagle', because it is so often mistaken for one. But the golden eagle's wing-span is 5-8 feet (1·5-2·4 m), double the buzzard's, and in flight its silhouette is rectangular, almost like a plank of wood. Golden eagles are found only in more remote areas and if you see one, it will be far away: consider yourself very lucky.

Buzzard feeding on rabbit

Watch and listen for grouse – large, ground-nesting game birds which make distinctive loud calls and, when disturbed, take off with an explosive whirring of wings. Red grouse favour open heather moorland, whereas black grouse prefer a mixture of this with woodland.

On higher ground you might see either of two colour-changing survivors from the last Ice Age: a ptarmigan is a mountain grouse whose plumage turns white in winter as camouflage against the snow. The mountain hare (*lepus timidus*) is a distinct species from brown hare, with shorter ears and a more rounded body. Its coat is brown in summer months, also turning white in winter.

Mountain hare

There is concern that shorter winters with less snow makes both ptarmigan and mountain hares vulnerable because their colour changes are not adapting to climate change.

Red grouse in heather (main) and black grouse (inset)

3

3·1 Drymen to Aberfoyle

Distance	10·8 miles 17·4 km
Terrain	minor road then forest tracks with some tarmac, followed by minor road and pavements into Aberfoyle
Grade	mostly easy or very easy, maximum height 210 m (690 ft) on road
Food and drink	Drymen, Aberfoyle
Side-trips	Scottish Wool Centre and Trossachs Discovery Centre, both in Aberfoyle
Summary	pleasant sheltered section mainly on forest tracks, passing many Victorian water supply features

```
00·0        3·9                        4·0              2·9      10·8
 O───────────O────────────────────────O────────────────O────────O
Drymen    6·3   Old Drymen Rd car park   6·4  Clashmore Cottage  4·7  Aberfoyle
```

- The Way leaves Drymen's main square on a minor road going north past the Clachan Inn* and passing Drymen Primary School. It becomes Old Gartmore Road, and also serves as Cycle Route 7 (NCN7).

- Follow the single-track road for a total of 3·9 miles (6·3 km) to Old Drymen Road car park. There are fine views to your right of the Campsie Fells, with the volcanic plug of Dumgoyne.

Clachan Inn, Drymen Square

- At mile 1·4, the West Highland Way crosses this road, but the Way keeps to the road, climbing steadily.

- After you pass Muir Park Reservoir and go under pylons, the mast on the right at mile 2·7 marks the highest point of this road. Ahead, the white houses of Gartmore contrast with the rugged Menteith Hills to the north.

- The road descends to reach Old Drymen Road car park at mile 3·9. The car park is on the right, opposite where the Way enters Loch Ard forest.

- Walkers turn left off the road taking the rightmost of the two tracks past a sign that prohibits unauthorised vehicles.

- Cyclists who prefer a flatter, smoother ride may prefer to stay on NCN7 which remains on the minor road to Aberfoyle (via Gartmore).

North from Old Drymen Road car park

- Follow the forest road through former woodland, on tarmac at first. To your right, the views feature Ben Ledi to the north-east and Ben Venue just west of north, with the rolling Menteith Hills in the foreground.

A typical domed shaft

- You are going through part of the huge Loch Katrine water scheme. Look for the rounded stones on your right that trace the line of the 1856-9 aqueduct, here running in a tunnel beneath your feet: see page 17.

- About mile 4·5 the road bends right and you pass a domed shaft on the left: see the photo above. These shafts were used for extracting spoil and for ventilation, and are a feature of today's section.

- At mile 5·2, you pass some houses and outbuildings, then pass a covered aqueduct and walkway running into a tunnel.

- Soon afterwards (mile 5·6) the road swings right and crosses a stream by a bridge with ironwork railings. It soon rises and you glimpse the impressive Corrie Aqueduct below, dating from 1859 and still in fine working order: see page 17.

- Just before the aqueduct, now protected by iron railings and completely covered, bear right on a narrow track with a loose surface. Stay to the right of the aqueduct and, where it crosses high above the Corrie Burn, notice the fine stonework of its pillars.

- After the aqueduct, the forest track climbs steadily, soon zigzagging uphill, crossing and re-crossing under the electricity pylons. Ignore a broad forest road that crosses the Way and continue uphill on the track. Behind you (south) there are fine views of the Campsies, terminating in the volcanic plug of Dumgoyne.

- Descend to a domed shaft at mile 7, a waymarked junction where you turn right. Cross a stream and generally descend for a further mile (1·6 km), perhaps glimpsing Clashmore Loch to your right, to Clashmore Cottage.

North-east over Clashmore Cottage

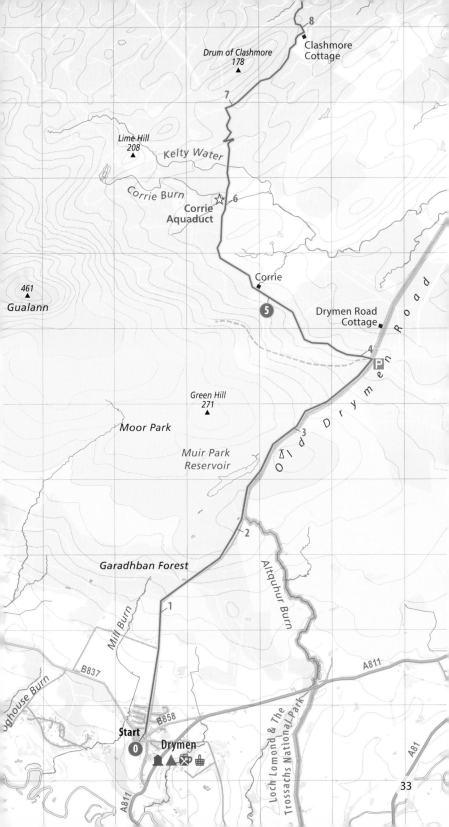

8

Clashmore
Cottage

Drum of Clashmore
178 ▲

7

Lime Hill
208 ▲

Kelty Water

Corrie Burn

Corrie
Aquaduct ☆ 6

Corrie

5

Drymen Road
Cottage

461 ▲
Gualann

4

Old Drymen Road

Green Hill
271 ▲

Moor Park

3

Muir Park
Reservoir

2

Garadhban Forest

Altquhur Burn

1

Mill Burn

B837

A811

oghouse Burn

B858

Start
0

Drymen

Loch Lomond & The
Trossachs National Park

A811

A811

33

Ben Lomond seen from Aberfoyle's main car park

- At the junction, turn sharp left uphill as waymarked. Within 400 m descend to another junction where you follow the main road around to the right, slightly uphill. You are joined on the left by a stream (the Bofrishlie Burn) that leads downhill and eventually into the Forth.

- Follow this road for the final two miles (3 km) out of the forest, ignoring various other minor tracks and, if it is still present, disregard a very misleading waymarker that seems to send you uphill to the right.

- Instead the Way sweeps downhill to the left. Emerge from the forest at Balleich, and continue along Manse Road for a further 0·8 miles (1·3 km) into Aberfoyle.

- Halfway along this section, note Kirkton Church and cemetery on your right. On either side of the entrance to the roofless church are two 'mort-safes' – heavy iron coffins designed to discourage body snatchers. The information board inside the church explains its interesting history.

- Manse Road takes you to the crossroads in Aberfoyle. Most of its facilities are to your right but a few B&Bs are to the left. The Riverside car park (on your right before the crossroads) houses the VisitScotland iCentre (tel 01877 381 221 and see page 78) and also the Scottish Wool Centre: see panel.

> **Scottish Wool Centre**
> Visitor centre featuring live sheepdog demonstrations (herding ducks) from April to September. Has shops, toilets and restaurant. Open daily year-round from 10 am: tel 01877 382 850.

The Trossachs

367 ▲

A821

Craig Leven
230 ▲

Brig
o' Turk

en Venue
29 ▲

Loch Achray

A821

16 ▲

Achray
Forest

333 ▲

387 ▲

A821

⌂

Loch
Ard

Milton

Dounans
Centre

11

12

Aberfoyle

Aberfoyle
Golf Club

Duchray Water

Lochan
Spling

☆ Kirkton
Church
(ruin)

10

River
Forth

Garbeg Hill ▲

9

A81

Bofrishlie Burn

⌂

△ ⛺
Cobleland

Arndrum
138 ▲

35

8

Drum of Clashmore
178 ▲

Clashmore
Cottage

3·2 Aberfoyle to Callander

Distance 9·9 miles (15·9 km)

Terrain mainly forest tracks, some stony paths and several streams to cross, sometimes boggy underfoot; forest tracks then minor road into Callander

Grade mainly gentle gradients with maximum height 220 m (720 ft) at the lochan, followed by descent to fairly flat roads for the final few miles

Food and drink Aberfoyle, Callander, also Kilmahog

Summary glorious walk through the Menteith hills, followed by a descent to Loch Venachar with fine views to the north

10·8							20·7
Aberfoyle	2·2 / 3·5	Braeval track	2·7 / 4·3	Lochan	3·0 / 4·8	Gartchonzie Bridge	2·0 / 3·2 Callander

- Return to the crossroads and go north up the A821 as signed; it's a right-left dogleg if you've come direct from Manse Road. Follow the A821 for 450 m, and after the last house, walkers take the stone steps on your right which then descend to join the cycleway. Cyclists continue for 50 m to the ironwork gates on NCN7, and read the notice about terrain and suitable bikes.

- Turn right to follow the cycleway into and through the forest. Within 500 m reach the footbridge across the Allt a' Mhangain ('the burn of the fawn'), with a waterfall to the left. Keep an eye out for red squirrels and roe deer in this part of the forest.

- Once across the footbridge, turn sharp right to follow the burn downstream (mile 11·4). After 800 m you are rejoined by a track coming up from Dounans Centre, which until 2021 the Way followed.

Footbridge across the Allt a' Mhangain

36

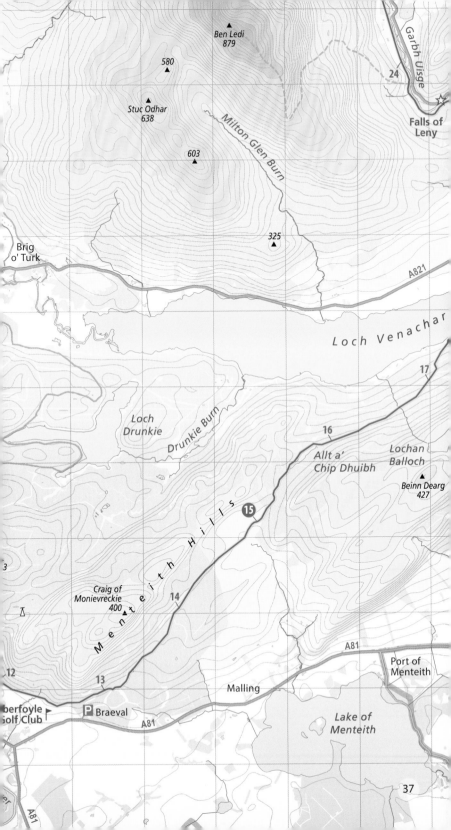

Garbh Uisge

Ben Ledi
879

580

24

Stuc Odhar
638

Falls of
Leny

603

Milton Glen Burn

Brig
o' Turk

325

A821

Loch Venachar

17

Loch
Drunkie

Drunkie Burn

16

Allt a'
Chip Dhuibh

Lochan
Balloch

15

Beinn Dearg
427

M e n t e i t h   H i l l s

3

Craig of
Monievreckie
400

14

A81

Port of
Menteith

12

13

Malling

berfoyle
Golf Club

P Braeval

A81

Lake of
Menteith

A81

37

- The road gradually gains height, lined by stately mature trees. To the right and behind you are picturesque views over Aberfoyle Golf Course and the Campsie Fells beyond.

- Follow the forest road, ignoring side tracks, and descend to a T-junction at mile 13 where you turn left up another forest road. (A right turn here would take you down to Braeval, a car park on the A81 that is useful for day visitors.)

- After nearly a mile on this broad stone-chipped forest road, it ends abruptly and the Way bears left down to a narrow winding path – after rain, perhaps boggy in places.

East along the forest road

- Descend through the final section of forest to emerge into an open section in which the outcrops of the rugged Menteith Hills become visible on your left. The tallest of these is Craig of Monievreckie at 400 m.

- Pass through a stone wall by a metal gate with a Malling Estate notice warning that Glenny Hill is a sheep grazing area and reminding dog owners of the need for close control. Continue ahead across rough pasture, with (in 2021) areas of clear felling. Stay alert for livestock.

- After a further 1 km, just beyond a stream crossing, follow the path that bears left uphill: see the photo below. Shortly afterwards, the Way passes through another stone wall by a metal gate.

Keep left uphill beyond the stream

Lochan Allt a' Chip Dhuibh

- Climb briefly through trees and, after you emerge, gain your first glimpse of the hills to the north. Descend on a twisting route through clear-felled forestry and newly planted saplings to the reed-fringed Lochan Allt a' Chip Dhuibh (mile 15·7).

- The lochan is rich in vegetation and home to fish and waterfowl. The Way starts along its left side, then veers away uphill to meet a forestry road at which you turn right. (If following the Way southbound, don't miss this narrow path down to the lochan: in 2021 its sign was as shown, with no RRW logo.)

- From the forest road you may see views of the hills to the north, with Ben Ledi high above Loch Venachar. Follow the road as it swings around the far end of the lochan with a boathouse. It's worth looking back from here for a view of the Menteith Hills.

- After a brief climb, for the next 1·5 miles (2·4 km) the track descends gradually towards the shore of Loch Venachar through a mixture of felled forestry and recent planting. En route you gain good views over the loch to the towering heights of Ben Ledi.

- The road drops steeply to a barrier: pass to its left to descend through the car park and reach the road. Turn right to leave Invertrossachs Estate through its East Lodge gateway.

- Follow the road along the south shore of Loch Venachar. Half a mile (800 m) after the end of the loch, a road on your left leads to Gartchonzie Bridge, a much-filmed bridge of great character, built in 1777 and still carrying vehicles (mile 18·7).

South-west over the Menteith Hills

Ben Ledi from Callander Meadows

🚲 • To bypass Callander, see below. For Callander itself, most cyclists will follow NCN7 along Invertrossachs Road and after 2 km turn left at the A81 into its centre. Walkers continue ahead around a bend and after 200 m, just after Wheels and the Trossachs Tryst, leave the road by turning right into Coilhallan Wood.

• Pass through the car park and follow the rough track uphill past a metal gate. It climbs through the wood with some glimpses of Ben Ledi to your left. Over a mile (1·8 km) after the car park, the track turns sharp right through some boulders, soon reaching a T-junction. Turn left and descend to reach the A81 within 450 m.

• Cross over and turn right, but within 50 m turn left on a footpath that descends to playing fields and reaches the River Teith. Turn right to cross the river by a narrow concrete footbridge (built in 1931) and reach the centre of Callander.

Track turns at boulders

To bypass Callander

• Turn left across Gartchonzie Bridge over the Eas Gobhain to reach the A821. Walkers cross the main road and pass through a timber gate past a Woodland Trust Scotland sign. Most cyclists will instead turn right to follow the main road for 1 km before turning left to resume NCN7.

• After the gate, follow the footpath (signed Great Trossachs Path) which curves uphill and then runs parallel to the road. After 1 km, exit the path through a tall gate and pass through Bochastle car park to pick up a path that runs beside the A821 until it reaches NCN7 northbound.

River Teith, Callander

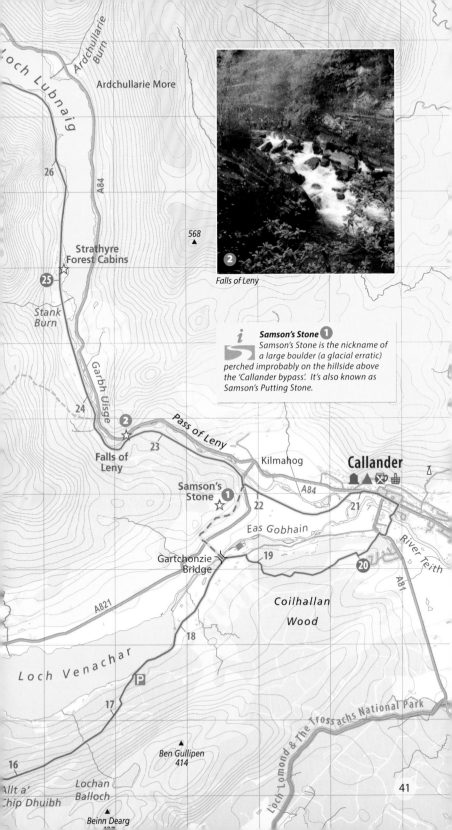

Loch Lubnaig

Ardchullarie Burn

Ardchullarie More

A84

26

568 ▲

Strathyre
Forest Cabins

25

Stank
Burn

Garbh Uisge

24

2

Pass of Leny

23

Falls of
Leny

Falls of Leny

i **Samson's Stone** ①

Samson's Stone is the nickname of
a large boulder (a glacial erratic)
perched improbably on the hillside above
the 'Callander bypass'. It's also known as
Samson's Putting Stone.

Kilmahog

Callander

A84

21

Samson's
Stone ①

22

Eas Gobhain

19

20

River Teith

Gartchonzie
Bridge

A81

Coilhallan

Wood

A821

18

Loch Venachar

P

17

Loch Lomond & The Trossachs National Park

16

Allt a'
Chip Dhuibh

Lochan
Balloch

Ben Gullipen
414 ▲

Beinn Dearg

41

3·3 Callander to Strathyre

Distance	9·2 miles 14·8 km
Terrain	good surface nearly all the way
Grade	easy, mainly flat cycleway following the trackbed of a dismantled railway, mostly well drained, some tarmac but also some muddy bits
Food and drink	Callander, Kilmahog, Strathyre
Side-trip	Ben Ledi: see page 23
Summary	easy section along the west shore of Loch Lubnaig, shared with the cycleway

Loch Lubnaig

20·7 1·5 2·7 3·4 1·6 29·9
Callander 2·4 bypass 4·4 5·4 2·6 Strathyre

- Leave Callander heading west by NCN7: it runs parallel to the main road (A84) just to its south, passing through the large car park and skateboard park before picking up the disused railway trackbed at mile 21·2. For about 2 km it is embanked above the Meadows and river flood plain with pleasant open views and some railway relics such as arches and old sleepers.

- At mile 22·2 you meet the A821: cross with care and continue on NCN7 for the next 7·5 miles (12 km) all the way to Strathyre. At first you are going upstream beside the Garbh Uisge – Gaelic for 'rough water'. The river's fast-flowing water can drown other sounds, so walkers and cyclists need to stay alert.

- The rapids culminate at mile 23·3 in the Falls of Leny, where torrents of white water tumble over massive rocks. To view the Falls, leave the cycleway at a rectangular concrete bench and turn right on a path for about 100 m before taking a steep path that drops towards the river, taking care near the fragile edges.

- Resume the cycleway afterwards, soon joining a minor road with car parking for the access path up Ben Ledi, where a minor road also joins from the A84. If you plan to climb Ben Ledi, see page 23 and follow the Mountain Code. Otherwise, keep ahead on the access road (marked 'private road') to Strathyre Forest Cabins (self-catering, but also with café, toilets and bike hire).

- The road ends at a gate where NCN7 continues on a rougher surface up the western shore of Loch Lubnaig to Strathyre. At mile 24·9 there's a path down to a lovely small beach with smooth boulders where you can sit and enjoy the loch's still, reflective waters. The name means 'the loch with a bend' – which you'll notice around mile 26·5.

NCN7 on disused railway trackbed

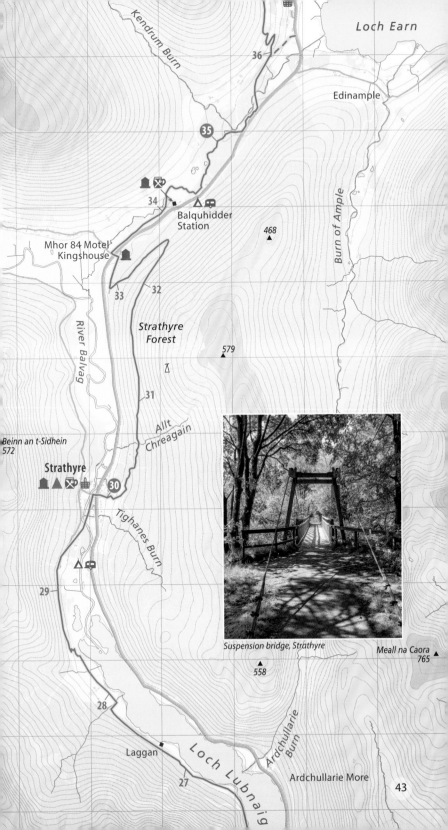

Loch Earn

36

Edinample

Kendrum Burn

35

Burn of Ample

34

Balquhidder
Station

468 ▲

Mhor 84 Motel
Kingshouse

33   32

River Balvag

Strathyre
Forest

579 ▲

31

Allt
Chreagain

Beinn an t-Sidhein
572

Strathyre

30

Tighanes Burn

29

Suspension bridge, Strathyre

Meall na Caora
765 ▲

558 ▼

28

Laggan

Loch Lubnaig

27

Ardchullarie More

Ardchullarie Burn

43

Loch Lubnaig – the 'loch with a bend'

- At mile 27·9 the route makes a right-left dogleg down closer to the shore, and after a further 800 m it makes a left-right before zigzagging steeply up to a track where you turn right. Below, the spit of land was deposited by the River Balvag, with little Lochan Buidhe between river and Way. This Site of Special Scientific Interest has outstanding riverine plant and animal life (e.g. azure damselfly and pearl mussel), and mixed woodland rich in bird life, including pied flycatchers.

- Cyclists who don't need the facilities of Strathyre now have a choice: you could stay on the minor road all the way from Strathyre for a 4-mile detour to Balquhidder to visit Rob Roy's grave: see page 15. The minor road rejoins the Way at mile 33·4 (Kingshouse). Alternatively from Strathyre you could stay on NCN7 which diverges from the busy A84 on its west side, rejoining the walking route at the same point.

- At mile 29·4 walkers descend gently to Strathyre along the minor road, looking out for the blue fingerpost at mile 29·7 which sends you briefly right down a road between two timber-clad houses (whilst NCN7 continues ahead). Immediately turn left and follow the tarmac path towards the village centre.

- Descend to and cross the suspension bridge shown on page 43. At its far side detour right to visit Strathyre's only café (The Broch) with tempting home baking. Otherwise go ahead across a lesser bridge and pass along the back of a row of houses to emerge in the centre of Strathyre, opposite the Ben Sheann hotel. Note that Strathyre has no public toilets.

South over Loch Lubnaig from near Strathyre

3·4 Strathyre to Killin

Distance	13·6 miles 21·9 km
Terrain	good forest track or road as far as Kingshouse; brief stretch of minor road, then good surface along the NCN7 cycleway to Killin
Grade	two steady climbs, the first gaining 150 m (490 ft) up through Strathyre Forest then descending steeply to Kingshouse; second ascent is to the top of Glen Ogle (gaining 200 m/ 655 ft), then descent to Killin
Food and drink	Strathyre, Kingshouse, Killin
Side-trip	Balquhidder (Rob Roy's grave), Lochearnhead
Summary	a varied day, with pleasant forest views over the meandering River Balvag, then splendid views eastward to Loch Earn

```
29·9      3·6         2·6        0·9              3·0          3·5   43·5
 O                                                     ●              O
Strathyre  5·8  Kingshouse  4·2    1·4            4·8    Lochan  5·7  Killin
                              Lochearnhead
```

- At the north of the village, signs point to the bridge where cyclists turn left to regain NCN7. Walkers turn right instead (between the former Munro Inn and Airlie House) through a car parking area. Walk up to the metal gate and turn left onto a path that passes a former church and goes to the right of a tennis court enclosure.

- Cross streams on two footbridges to climb on a narrow path through forest. After 500 m, meet a broad forest road and turn left to follow it for the next 3 miles. (Southbound walkers need to look out carefully for this junction.)

- Coninue ahead, bearing right uphill where a road bears left downhill. Enjoy views across the valley to Beinn an t-Sidhean (Ben Sheann). After a while the forestry road levels out, with views over the River Balvag meandering through the valley to your left.

Upper footbridge leading into the forest

West towards Beinn an t-Sidhean

- After a quarry on your right, start the long descent to Kingshouse, ignoring a forest road that bears right uphill. You may glimpse white buildings through the trees below, but the forest road veers north-east then hairpins south-west. Finally it swings back down to Kingshouse.

- At the bottom of the forestry road, you meet the old A84 at right angles: turn right for the Mhor 84 motel with bar, café and restaurant.

- From the motel, go under the A84 on the minor road towards Balquhidder. (To visit Rob Roy's grave from here is a distance of 1·8 miles/2·9 km each way.) To continue the Way, instead turn right just after the underpass at the NCN7 sign to Killin.

Mhor 84 Motel, Kingshouse

East over Loch Earn from the Way

- The cycleway takes you parallel to the A84, rather close to it for the first two miles. Some streams help to drown the traffic noise in places, but it is a pleasant relief when it swings away from the road, soon crossing a large bridge across Glen Kendrum. A stone commemorates the young music teacher who died in 1997 while cycling on the A9.

- The cycleway starts to climb, gently at first, then steeply through a series of hairpin bends. The village of Lochearnhead lies well below you: to visit it, see the panel below. Otherwise keep climbing, enjoying the views of Loch Earn to your right.

- Leaving Loch Earn behind, the Way veers left and enters Glen Ogle, towards its superb long viaduct. Soon afterwards, notice the ivy-clad bridge numbered 116, surrounded by mossy, dripping rocks. For more about this railway, see page 19.

Diversion to Lochearnhead

This detour involves losing 80 m of altitude to the A84 and later climbing back steeply to regain 150 m. It is useful mainly if you are overnighting in Lochearnhead.

At mile 36, just before going under a road bridge, bear right along a well-signed concrete path to reach a minor road. Bear right down the road which meets the main road just beyond St Angus' Church. Turn left along the pavement for 600 m past the village store (the only source of daytime food in Lochearnhead). At the main T-junction, turn right for the village.

After your visit, return to this T-junction and continue north on the left side of the main road (now the A85). The pavement soon gives way to grass and you bear left up the drive towards Lochearnhead Scout Station. Just past its entrance, look for the sign below and turn right up the Glen Ogle Trail. Go through the tall kissing-gate, turn right and follow a waymarked uphill path, steep and rocky in parts, with many tree roots. At the top of this strenuous climb, turn right onto NCN7.

- Two km after the viaduct, you pass a lochan on your left: see the photo below. This lochan has rare plant life, including the Least Yellow Water-lily, rare sedges, mosses and bladderworts.

- Just afterwards, follow NCN7 signs to cross the A85 (with care) to a car park with picnic tables. Continue uphill past a memorial to two RAF Tornado pilots killed in 1994.

- Go through the gate to continue the cycleway, ignoring the forest road uphill to the right – unless bypassing Killin: see below.

Memorial to the RAF pilots who died in 1994

- The Way now starts to descend towards the main road, but soon it veers away and becomes more peaceful. After the tarmac surface ends at two bollards, the Way bends to the right. It becomes a pleasant forest road embanked in places and with low bridges over streams that feature fine old stonework.

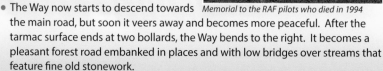

Alternative: bypass Killin

Turn right up the forest road (bullet three above), and follow it uphill for about 4 miles until you reach the junction with a mast: see page 51, last bullet. This saves several miles and a lot of ascent and descent, but means that you miss the attractions of Killin.

Lochan Lairig Cheile

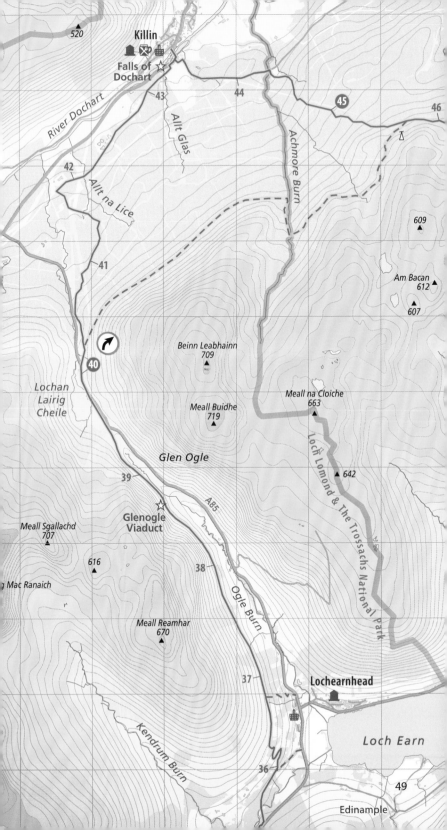

Falls of Dochart, Killin

- At a T-junction, turn left downhill and 750 m later turn right to pick up the trackbed of an old railway. Approaching Killin, join the A827 just before reaching the Falls of Dochart on the left. Across the river, the restored watermill is now a house. This part of Breadalbane was once the stronghold of the Clan MacNab, and their ancient burial ground still survives on the island of Inchbuie just below the falls. For more on this fascinating area, visit *www.visitbreadalbane.org*.

- Cross the bridge to reach the village centre with some attractive facilities. Or continue the Way by turning right along the South Loch Tay road just before Bridge of Dochart.

St Fillan's Mill, Killin

3·5 Killin to Ardtalnaig

Distance	11·9 miles (19·2 km)
Terrain	minor road then rough track, followed by faint sheep paths then farm road, ending with three miles of undulating South Loch Tay road
Grade	long steady ascent from Killin (at 120 m/390 ft) to high mast (altitude 565 m/1850 ft) followed by long descent to return to Loch Tay at 120 m
Food and drink	Killin, Ardeonaig Hotel (see page 55)
Summary	a splendid cross-country section past Lochan Breaclaich with fine views over Loch Tay; compass useful; can be exposed in adverse conditions

Achamore Burn — South Loch Tay Road

43·5	0·9		2·5 Lochan Breaclaich	2·9 Pipeline	2·5		3·1	55·4
Killin	1·5	4·1		4·6	4·0	Ardeonaig	5·0	**Ardtalnaig**

- Turn right up the South Loch Tay road (opposite the Falls of Dochart) and follow it for 0·9 miles (1·5 km) to the Achmore Burn.

- Most cyclists will prefer to follow NCN7 all the way to Kenmore and beyond: see panel.

- Walkers turn right immediately after the low bridge onto a private tarmac road and follow it as it climbs steadily. After 1·2 miles (2 km) reach tall gates with notices about vehicle access and stalking. The two patches of water far ahead are both part of Loch Tay.

- Within 200 m you are joined from the right by a forest road – the 'Killin bypass': see page 48. You may wish to detour briefly up to the tall mast which stands at 400 m/1300 ft. Here is a splendid view all round, including, on a clear day, to Ben Lui (1130 m) some 25 miles away to the west: see foot of page 53.

NCN7 from Killin to Pitlochry

NCN7 runs traffic-free as far as the Falls of Dochart, then turns right along the South Loch Tay public road to and through Kenmore.

From there it heads north-east across River Lyon and cyclists can use the B846 to reach Weem (just north of Aberfeldy). NCN7 continues on road north of River Tay all the way to Pitnacree where it crosses the River Tay to Grandtully and continues on road to re-cross the Tay to Logierait. It follows a mixture of minor road and forest track towards Pitlochry via Dunfallandy, and rejoins the Way to cross River Tummel on the footbridge. Visit **bit.ly/RR-ncn7** for detailed mapping.

Bridge of Dochart, with Tarmachan ridge behind

West over Lochan Breaclaich

- Resuming the main Way, follow the undulating access road, on tarmac at first. There are fine views behind you, perhaps of the twin peaks of Ben More and Stob Binnein about 15 miles to the south-west and often snow-capped into summer. At 1174 m (3851 ft), Ben More is the highest point in Stirlingshire.

- One mile (1·6 km) after the gate reach the impressive Breaclaich Dam, which turned a small lochan into a major power source. It provides efficient hydro-electricity, driving three separate power stations on its way downhill.

- Follow the rough track around the northern edge of Lochan Breaclaich, past the quarry that provided stone for the dam. The track continues its climb around the shoulder of Creag Gharbh, then swings sharply right to reach the summit of the Way at 565 m/1850 ft.

- From here, the track descends continuously, swinging left around the shoulder of Meall Odhar. As you approach the tiny Lochan a' Chaorainn (on your right), you glimpse Loch Tay ahead and the Way descends north-easterly towards the loch.

- About 1 km after the lochan, the Way meets a huge water pipeline which briefly you walk beside. After 200 m the pipeline turns right: leave it to head downhill.

The Way passes beside the pipeline

Holly Cottage

Ardtalnaig
Kindrochit
Ardtalnaig Burn

Claggan

Allt Chloidh

Shee of Ardtalnaig

56

55

54

(The) Old Manse

53

Ardeonaig

52

Allt a' Mheinn

Newton Burn

Finglen Burn

Tullich Hill
682

Meall nan Oighreag
833

Lawers

L o c h   T a y

A827

FB

ae
m

Meall Daimh

West over Breachlaich: Stob Binnein, Ben More & Ben Lui

Descend between two patches of conifers

- Follow a sequence of tall yellow-topped waymarker posts over rough pasture on narrow paths across a couple of stream crossings and boggy areas, aiming towards Loch Tay between two patches of conifers. Pass ruined sheilings on your way down to the gate in the stone wall at the northmost corner of the lower, rectangular patch of woodland.

- From this gate, head for 650 m towards the farm buildings visible below (NNE). The narrow path finally picks up a farm track that fords the Newton Burn.

- Take the timber footbridge on the left and continue to descend the farm track (with Newton Burn now on your right) to reach Brae Farm within 700 m.

Ben Lawers towers over Loch Tay

The gate above Brae Farm

North-east over Loch Tay

- Exit Brae Farm and descend on a single-track road past two cottages. The minor road continues past the Abernethy Trust Outdoor Centre and within a mile meets the South Loch Tay road at the Ardeonaig Hotel with (disused) red phone box and defibrillator.

- Visit the hotel for walker-friendly meals, or continue the Way by turning right for the final 3 miles (5 km) to Ardtalnaig.

- At first you climb noticeably (to around 180 m/600 ft), passing the boundary sign for Perth & Kinross near The Old Manse. After some fine views of Loch Tay and the mountains behind, you descend all the way to Ardtalnaig past Kindrochit House (B&B in garden flat).

The Ardeonaig Hotel

- To follow the Glen Quaich extension, turn right at the disused phone box at Ardtalnaig: see page 70. To continue the Way, stay on the road across the Ardtalnaig Burn, within 500 m passing Holly Cottage (with B&B in pods in its garden).

3·6 Ardtalnaig to Aberfeldy

Distance	14·6 miles 23·5 km
Terrain	tarmac at first, then rough paths and farm tracks, followed by gorge path with timber steps and boardwalk in steep parts
Grade	minor road at first, then steep ascent, followed by undulating ridge-walk (maximum height 1150 ft/350 m) and long descent through the Birks
Food and drink	Aberfeldy only (unless diverting to Kenmore: see below)
Side-trips	Scottish Crannog Centre; Dewar's Aberfeldy Distillery
Summary	a scenic day with rewarding views from a ridge linking two fine gorges; could be split, e.g. by overnighting at Kenmore

55·4		4·7	Acharn	3·3	Tombuie Cottage	3·7	forest path	2·9		70·0
Ardtalnaig		7·5		5·3		6·0		4·7		**Aberfeldy**

- From Ardtalnaig, the Way runs along the South Loch Tay road all the way to Acharn (4·7 miles/7·5 km). Although a 'walking/cycling friendly road', be aware that its 40 mph speed limit is only advisory, and sight lines are poor in places.

- Unless cycling (see panel on page 51) or taking the diversion into Kenmore (see panel opposite), walkers turn right at the 'Falls of Acharn circular walk' sign.

- Follow the gravelly road uphill beside the Acharn Burn, which you'll hear long before you can see it. After 700 m, turn left at the sign to the Hermit's Cave, a theatrical folly built by John Campbell, third Earl of Breadalbane, in the 1760s.

- Once inside the folly, let your eyes adapt to the dark. Turn left and step down to enjoy the glorious view from the platform.
Originally this was enclosed, featuring a bow window overlooking the main falls, with stuffed wild animals in niches around the cave walls.

> ### Diversion into Kenmore
> *From Acharn to the beach at Kenmore is only 1·5 miles/2·4 km along the South Loch Tay road, passing the Scottish Crannog Centre's current site: see page 21. Kenmore has a range of accommodation and places to eat, and has the imposing entrance to Taymouth Castle which dates from 1810.*
>
> *To rejoin the Way after Kenmore, turn up the Glen Quaich road from its junction with the A827, then follow the steep zigzags for a further 1·2 miles (2 km) to Tombuie Cottage: resume from page 59 bullet one.*

North over Loch Tay from the Way

Fortingall

Croftgarrow

River Lyon

Tay Forest Park

Drummond Hill
460

Scottish
Crannog
Centre
from 2022
☆

A827

Fearnan

L o c h   T a y

Remony

60

Acharn

Falls of
Acharn
☆

59

Achianich Burn

58

Acharn Burn

57

Beinn Bhreac
716

658

56

🏠 Holly Cottage

Ardtalnaig

Kindrochit

55

Ardtalnaig Burn

Tullichglass (ruin)

Claggan

Allt Chloidh

Shee of Ardtalnaig

Gleann a' Chilleine

57

Creagan na Beinne
888

Tullich Hill

Falls of Acharn

- After viewing the falls, turn left to leave the cave by its upper exit. Continue up the track until it crosses the Acharn Burn by a timber army-built bridge with fine views over the cascades.

- Once across the bridge, turn right uphill and follow the farm road as it passes through gates and swings left, settling into an easterly direction. The road has a grassy centre and passes the Queen's Wood enclosed by its fine old drystone wall.

- Shortly after the wood, a fingerpost points to an optional half-mile detour up to a stone circle. Otherwise cross the Remony Burn by a gated timber footbridge, and turn left on its far side.

- The Way passes through a metal gate, and follows the broad track known as the Queen's Drive ever since Queen Victoria admired the fine views of Loch Tay and Schiehallion from her horse-drawn carriage some 180 years ago.

- Descend past the farm buildings and house at Balmacnaughton on your left. Further on, the path narrows and passes through a gate leading into Bolfracks Estate through mixed woodland with birch, rowan and oak.

Footbridge over the Remony Burn

- After about a mile within Bolfracks, you approach a tall gate leading to the Glen Quaich road. Either exit here and turn right up the road for 700 m to Tombuie Cottage, or save 500 m of road-walking by turning right before the gate. Follow the estate's Kenmore Hill Walk, then Larch Walk, to emerge through a car park and turn right up the road for just 200 m.

- At Tombuie Cottage, pass through the gate at its left and follow the farm road for half a mile as it descends across a burn, past Tombuie House and towards a patch of conifer forest.

- Just short of the forest gate, turn right at the huge white ROB ROY WAY sign up a very narrow path. Go through a fence and within 100 m join a broad estate road. Follow it to and through tall metal gates.

- The trees thin out in places and you see Tower House (self-catering) in a gap to your left. Emerge onto an open section along a grassy road with good views over the broad valley of the Tay.

Tower House

- Afterwards pass through gates into a deer-fenced plantation, crossing the Croftmoraig Burn and emerging at Tullichuil. Follow the forest road as it veers right and climbs steeply around a tall pylon carrying power lines.

- Just after you draw level with the pylon, go left on a broad timber extraction road and over a cattle-grid. Within 100 m, at a discreet sign bear left to continue on a narrower track under the power lines. There are good views of Schiehallion from this section.

North-west from the Way to Schiehallion

Bear left on a narrower track

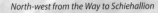

- Soon re-enter forest and after 750 m, just after a vehicle turning space, look for a waymarker that sends you steeply down a narrow grassy path bearing left. Soon pass under further power lines, go through a gate and emerge from the trees.

- The views open out below, and you may be able to pick out Aberfeldy with its Wade bridge ahead. However the Way soon detours via the Birks and there's over 2·5 fairly strenuous miles (over 4 km) still to go.

- Descend the grassy track, at first beside the ruins of a stone wall, as it winds down to a handsome stone house at Upper Farrochil. Walk down its access road almost as far as the farm buildings at Dunskiag.

Bear left down a narrow path

- Just before Dunskiag, spot the fingerpost on the right. (Following 'Aberfeldy 1 mile' to the left instead offers a major shortcut, handy if you are running out of daylight.) However the Way turns right towards The Birks on a track that climbs for nearly a mile to 285 m before passing under pylons and emerging though a gate to to meet Urlar Road.

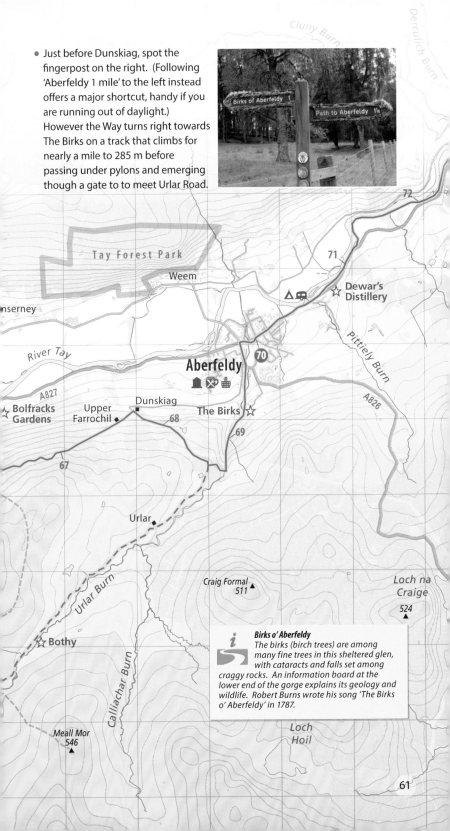

Birks o' Aberfeldy
The birks (birch trees) are among many fine trees in this sheltered glen, with cataracts and falls set among craggy rocks. An information board at the lower end of the gorge explains its geology and wildlife. Robert Burns wrote his song 'The Birks o' Aberfeldy' in 1787.

- At the road, turn right briefly uphill, but within 50 m turn left on a footpath with a discreet marker post. This path is where the Glen Quaich extension rejoins the main Way.

- The Birks is a splendid wooded gorge formed over several millennia by the scouring action of ice and water, in this case the Moness Burn. Although you follow it downhill only, the terrain is challenging in places, with undulations and some slippery steps.

Discreet marker on path to The Birks

- Follow the path until you can turn right across the bridge where the Way goes over the Moness Burn. There are paths down both sides of the gorge, but the Way descends on its east side to pass a viewing platform over the dramatic upper falls.

- Lower down, just after a handrail section, is Burns' seat: see below. Here in 1787 the poet was inspired to write his song *The Birks o' Aberfeldy*. Verses from it are carved in various places.

- Near the bottom of the path, after many rapids and side-falls, you pass the Burns statue seated on a bench. Afterwards cross the burn again by footbridge and turn right to reach an open area with picnic tables and car park below.

Upper falls of the Moness Burn

Robert Burns' stone seat in The Birks

Here Robert Burns was inspired to write *The Birks of Aberfeldy.*

- Take the footpath on the left of road and car park down to the busy A826. Cross straight over with care, and go through a gap in the wall to follow a woodland path at first beside the Moness Burn. Cross it by footbridge and pass through the Lower Birks Park, an area regenerated in 2018 by a collaborative project.

- You emerge at Aberfeldy's Square, which has eateries, shops, a cinema and the Breadalbane Arms. This is Scotland's first Fair Trade Town and it features Wade's favourite bridge: see pages 14-15.

Statue of Robert Burns, The Birks

The Square is home to an ornate cast-iron drinking fountain – gifted by Gavin, Marquis of Breadalbane 'as a memento of the cordial reception accorded to him & Lady Breadalbane by the inhabitants … after the restoration of the Marquisate, July 1885'.

A notable Aberfeldy institution is the Watermill, in Mill Street. Housed in a superbly restored watermill are an excellent bookshop, art gallery and coffee shop, with Homer homeware shop, open year-round: *www.aberfeldywatermill.com.*

Historic drinking fountain

3·7 Aberfeldy to Pitlochry

Distance	9·3 miles 15·0 km
Terrain	riverside path and disused railway trackbed, then informal uphill path with boggy bits across open moorland, finally forest tracks almost all the way
Grade	low-level flattish paths at first, then steady ascent to 1150 ft/350 m followed by moderate descent into Pitlochry
Food and drink	Aberfeldy, Strathtay (small shop), Pitlochry
Side-trips	Visitor Centre and other attractions, Pitlochry
Summary	after the easy first five miles, follow an ancient Right of Way through moorland and forest, past a stone circle, to finish in the centre of Pitlochry

70·0	2·5 disused railway	2·6 Strathtay	2·0 Stone circle	2·2	79·3
Aberfeldy 4·1	4·2	3·2	3·5		Pitlochry

- From Aberfeldy's Square head east beside the A827 main road. After 900 m, Dewar's Distillery is on your right: see below.

- Just beyond the cemetery on your left, follow the timber fingerpost pointing along the footpath beside the road.

- At mile 71·3 the path heads down toward the River Tay to follow its south bank: enjoy some fine riverside views with plenty of water birds. Road noise recedes, and the path is punctuated by metal gates and a timber footbridge.

- After a further mile or so, the footpath bears right uphill to the embanked trackbed of the old railway line. Follow it all the way to Grandtully, with the river on your left and A827 on your right, sometimes in cuttings.

Former railway trackbed

i **Dewar's Aberfeldy Distillery**
www.dewars.com
Established in 1898, it offers tours with tastings and audio guide (eight languages). Audiovisual show, café, e-postcard kiosk, nature trail and steam train. Open year-round: tel 01887 822 010.

Loch
Derculich

Tullypowrie Burn

76

Cluny Burn

Derculich Burn

75

Strathtay

74

Grandtully

River Tay

Little
Ballinluig

73

72

Westpark Burn

387 ▲

71

★ Dewar's
Distillery

Pittrely Burn

Cultullich Burn

A826

Loch
Scoly

Grandtully Hill
532 ▲

Loch
Kennard

477
▲

Loch na
Craige

524
▲

65

Rafting on the Tay at Grandtully

- After a further 2 mi/3 km approach Grandtully, marked by noise from the nearby main road: ignore it and keep to the trackbed all the way to the village centre.

- Pass through a railway arch to emerge at the Old Station Yard (the campsite of the Scottish Canoe Association). Turn left across the yard and continue to the A827 where you turn right for 100 m.

- Cross the River Tay by the metal bridge on your left: take care because there's no pavement. You may see canoes on the river, running its rapids and weaving through slalom gates.

- Beyond the river, you face Strathtay's War Memorial where you turn right along the road past Bendarroch Guest House. (Keep ahead to detour via the village store and post office.)

- Within 300 m you join the village road that runs beside the golf course. Cross diagonally right towards the red phone box, and turn left up the lane (fingerpost 'Public Footpath to Pitlochry'). On entering the golf club, immediately look for a low sign pointing right uphill.

Sign in gorse, just after tall gate

- At first, the walk feels pleasantly enclosed by dry-stone walls, with overhanging oak, beech and birch. You climb steadily, passing through various gates to emerge into open farmland with sheep grazing. Stay to the right of gorse bushes approaching Tullypowrie Burn.
- Continue uphill with the burn on your right for about 1 km until you see a footbridge, and turn right across it. On its far side, continue uphill across a steep boggy bit for about 100 m.
- Reach a fence on your right and follow it for 70 m before going through a tall gate. On the left, a timber sign points the way to Pitlochry: it may be hard to spot because it's low among gorse. Follow its line and emerge from the gorse.
- You now follow a bearing of 060° (east-north-east) across pathless moorland for over 1 km. In good conditions, this may be easy to navigate, but in poor visibility you need map and compass skills. Refer to map page 68.
- Aim uphill on the same heading towards a corner of the plantation ❶. Approach it, but stay about 50 m short of it to avoid gorse bushes, and cross a stream.
- At the end of this bit of plantation, reach a fence and pass through the gap at its left end. Just beyond you will see the fine Scots pine shown at mile 76·4 see ❷ on page 68.
- Stay on the same heading of 060° for a further 500 m to approach the corner of Fonab Forest. Pass through the tall gate about 70 m to the left of its corner ❸. Before you enter the forest, look behind you for glorious views south-west to Ben Lawers: see the photo on pages 22-23.
- Follow the forest road north-easterly, ignoring a left turn after 400 m. After a further 150 m, look left for an ancient stone circle standing aloof and mysterious. You can go up close to these 3600-year old stones, but please don't touch them. The four-poster circle is about 5 m in diameter, with fragments of the fourth stone buried in the ground.

Clachan an Diridh, near mile 77

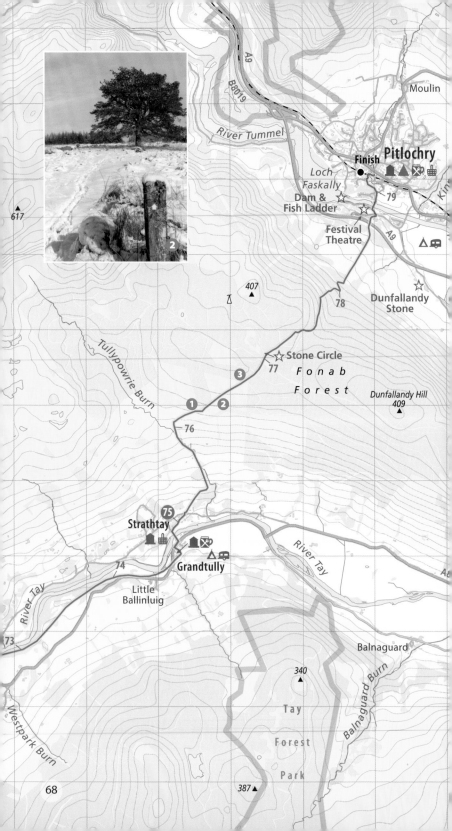

Moulin

River Tummel

Pitlochry

Finish

Loch
Faskally

Dam &
Fish Ladder

79

Kin...

617

Festival
Theatre

A9

Dunfallandy
Stone

78

407

Stone Circle

77

Fonab

3

Forest

Dunfallandy Hill
409

Tullypowrie Burn

1

2

76

Strathtay

75

River Tay

A8...

74

Grandtully

Little
Ballinluig

73

Balnaguard

River Tay

Balnaguard Burn

340

Tay

Westpark Burn

Forest

Park

68

387

- Within a further 200 m, you reach a crossroads with a timber signpost. Go straight over on the narrow grassy path and follow brownish signs to Pitlochry via the Clunie Walk. At first the Way runs alongside another forest road, then crosses it and descends alongside a burn.

- Emerge from Fonab Forest by a kissing-gate, and turn right to descend the minor road as it zigzags downhill past farm buildings. Cross the A9, Scotland's main north-south highway, with great care (fast-moving traffic).

- Go straight ahead through the gate down a lane, soon crossing Foss Road, angling left. The Way now bears left towards Port-na-Craig.

- Before turning right to cross the footbridge, consider a detour to visit the dam, with a famous fish ladder used by 250,000 salmon. Go straight ahead past the Festival Theatre to the dam's Visitor Centre which opens daily, entry free: *www.pitlochrydam.com*.

- The Way continues across the River Tummel by its fine suspension bridge, which in 1913 replaced the ferry that had plied there since the 12th century. Its wobbles may be slightly unsettling, but it gives fine views and an information board explains the bridge and its opening.

- Keep ahead on the path between houses and playing fields, and cross straight over Tummell Crescent onto a narrow footpath. This winds north-west through Bobbin Mill Wood. Cross Ferry Road with Pay & Display car park on the right, and pass through the arch under the railway bridge with a stream on your right.

- Turn right across the footbridge on a path that leads into the back corner of the Memorial Garden that marks the end of the Way. The War Memorial stands on Atholl Road, Pitlochry's main street; turn right for its VisitScotland iCentre.

- Congratulations on completing the Way. This may be time to reflect on all you've experienced since leaving Drymen, and the changes in landscapes and lifestyles since Rob Roy's lifetime.

Pitlochry Memorial Garden

3·8 Ardtalnaig to Moness via Glen Quaich 72 73 74 75 77

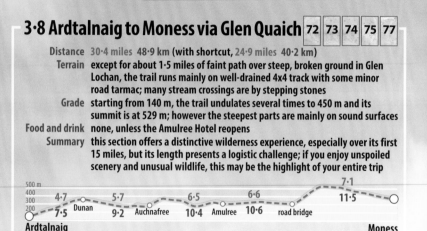

Distance	**30·4 miles 48·9 km (with shortcut, 24·9 miles 40·2 km)**
Terrain	except for about 1·5 miles of faint path over steep, broken ground in Glen Lochan, the trail runs mainly on well-drained 4x4 track with some minor road tarmac; many stream crossings are by stepping stones
Grade	starting from 140 m, the trail undulates several times to 450 m and its summit is at 529 m; however the steepest parts are mainly on sound surfaces
Food and drink	none, unless the Amulree Hotel reopens
Summary	this section offers a distinctive wilderness experience, especially over its first 15 miles, but its length presents a logistic challenge; if you enjoy unspoiled scenery and unusual wildlife, this may be the highlight of your entire trip

500 m
400
300
200

7·1
4·7   5·7   6·5   6·6   11·5
7·5   Dunan   9·2 Auchnafree 10·4 Amulree 10·6 road bridge

Ardtalnaig   **Moness**

Even using the shortcut, the shortest distance is 24·9 miles (40·2 km) and unless you can yomp that in a single day, you would need to organise collection from Amulree to reach somewhere with food and lodging – probably Aberfeldy.

If time is short, we suggest you consider doing the first half only: it is a superb wilderness experience with no turbines and hardly any road-walking. That way you need only one taxi or lift from Amulree to Aberfeldy (11·3 miles on the A822) to resume the main Way. Note that you would need to pre-arrange a collection time at Amulree where you may have doubtful mobile reception.

- From Ardtalnaig's former phone box turn right up the single-track road which climbs steeply away from the loch. Look behind you for fine views over Loch Tay and the hills beyond.

- After nearly a mile, the road bends left across a metal bridge and continues to climb towards Claggan farmhouse. Just before the farm, the Way turns left as signed onto a moorland track.

- After you pass the ruins at Tullichglass the track swings right into Gleann a' Chilleine, still climbing. At a point where the burn crosses the track, you can avoid wet feet by a short detour left to an improvised footbridge.

Improvised footbridge

North-west over Loch Tay

Sheep posing on a fine drumlin

- You may start noticing the effects of glaciation, including the U-shaped valley with scattered boulders (or erratics) left by an east-flowing glacier during the last Ice Age. Grassy drumlins (rounded humps left behind by the glacier) are a prominent feature of this section.

- After levelling out at a height of 425 m, descend gently to the boarded up cottage at Dunan where the track fades out. Pass between the cottage and the stone sheepfold to pick up a fainter track, grassy at first, stony later. It descends the valley of the infant River Almond with the river to your right.

- Upper Glen Almond is a glorious wilderness experience with few signs of human settlement and no pylons,

Dunan

turbines or others intrusions. Signs of glaciation are everywhere, with unusually fine drumlins. After over a mile of descent, the first reminder of human activity is a dam with fish ladder.

West over the dam, River Almond

71

- You pass several ruined farm buildings, and just after the Stuck Chapel Burn there's a war memorial to victims of World War 1. The absence of any World War 2 names underlines the extent of rural depopulation.

- Lower down, pass among some houses and bear left up towards Auchnafree. Once through its gate, turn right through a stand of trees, then left past the barn, to pass through two gates. Be aware of vehicles turning in this area.

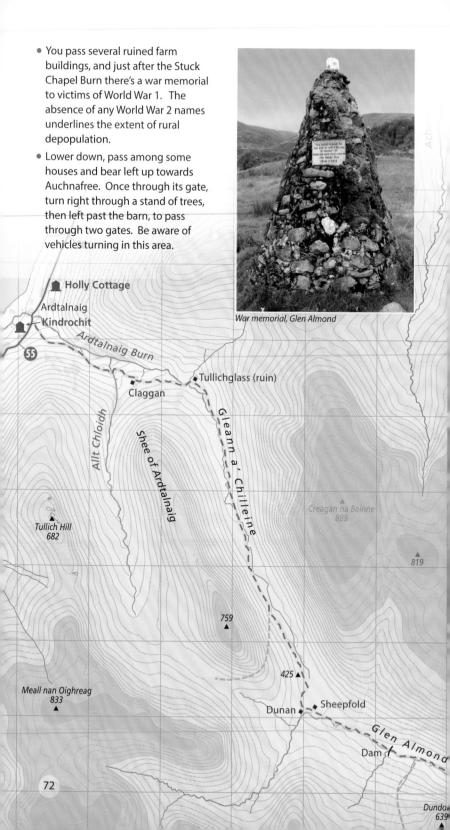

War memorial, Glen Almond

🏠 **Holly Cottage**

Ardtalnaig

Kindrochit

55

Ardtalnaig Burn

Tullichglass (ruin)

Claggan

Allt Chloidh

Shee of Ardtalnaig

Gleann a' Chilleine

Creagan na Beinne
888

Tullich Hill
682

819

759

425

Meall nan Oighreag
833

Dunan

Sheepfold

Glen Almond

Dam

Achc

Dunda
639

- Stay on the track which now climbs above the Glenshervie Burn. After about 350 m, descend to cross the burn. In 2021 the decrepit railway sleeper footbridge had a modern alternative to its left.

- On the far side of the bridge, turn sharp right on a narrow, barely discernible trod path. Follow it up into a steep-sided gully up to Glen Lochan.

- This narrow defile runs over broken ground and you may have to cross the burn several times to find the best route, using heather for hand-holds in places. Soon, a better path runs above the saddle, up to the right.

- Descending from over 440 m, the path passes a few tiny lochans and the ruins of an old fence. Climb the hillside

South towards Auchnafree from near the saddle

  diagonally to the left to pick up a rough 4x4 track that makes easier going than the boggy lower ground.

- The track climbs briefly, then descends to the shore of reed-fringed Lochan a' Mhuilinn with its fishing hut. Follow the track all the way down to Croftmill with views of Loch Freuchie ahead.

- At the single-track road the Way turns right and follows it to the A822 where it turns left towards Amulree before returning on Loch Freuchie's northern side. The A822 is a suitable place to be collected by a vehicle, although the single-track road also has a long lay-by just 300 m short of Croftmill which saves 2·4 miles of road-walking. (Never park in a passing place, no matter how briefly.)

- Alternatively, if yomping this section in a single day, consider turning left instead to bypass Amulree, within 1·8 km rejoining the Way heading north-west. This shortcut reduces the total distance by 5·5 miles/8·9 km.

Amulree Church

Beach at the north-west end of Loch Freuchie

- To complete the section, just after Amulree Church and former hotel (a building site in 2021), bear left down a short lane with bollards to cross the River Braan and turn left onto the private road.

- This runs on tarmac as far as Lochan Lodge, then on a rougher surface around the north side of Loch Freuchie to reach the Turrerich Burn, with good views to your left.

- Cross the burn by timber bridge, pass the farm and perhaps detour to the lovely beach at the end of the loch. Cross the River Quaich by a two-arched stone bridge and after 250 m, turn right at the tarmac road and follow it for nearly 1 mile to Auchnacloich.

- Leave the road by turning right to re-cross the River Quaich and follow the track past Wester Shian and Tirchardie. After 1·7 miles, emerge on the road just after its hump-backed bridge over the river.

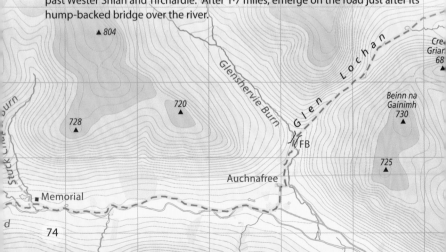

South-east over Glen Quaich

Turrerich

Glenfender Burn

C r a i g

552 ▲

H u l i c h

Loch Freuchie

Lochan
Lodge

Croftmill

River Braan

Amulree
Church ✝

Allt Mhuilinn

Glen Quaich Road

Lochan a'
Mhuillin

A822

Crom Chreag
479
▲

▲ 704

Corrymuckloch

686
▲

75

Meall Reamhar
667
▲

Schiehallion from the Glen Quaich road

- Continue up the road that climbs steeply, with fine views behind you over Glen Quaich and Loch Freuchie: see page 75.

- You know that you have topped out (at 529 m) once shapely Schiehallion starts to appear ahead: see photo above.

- Within 0·6 miles the road descends to a small reservoir. Turn sharp right across the fence (in 2021 by a rickety stile) onto a stony track just before the reservoir.

- Follow the track for 1·1 miles to a Y-junction where you bear right. Within 0·9 miles reach a T-junction with a utility road and turn left briefly. Within 50 m turn right under power lines to continue down beside the Urlar Burn.

- After a further 800 m there's a charming estate bothy on the right, by tradition unlocked. If you use it, please leave it exactly as you find it.

- About 1·2 miles after the bothy you approach Urlar Farm. Go through the signed gate on the right, cross a field to pass through the next gate and turn left on a narrow path between fence and low trees.

- The path soon rejoins the farm road which you follow for 0·6 miles, passing a square reservoir, to meet the main route: see the top of page 62. Turn right into woodland on the path to the Falls of Moness, resuming the Way to Aberfeldy.

Bothy near the Urlar Burn

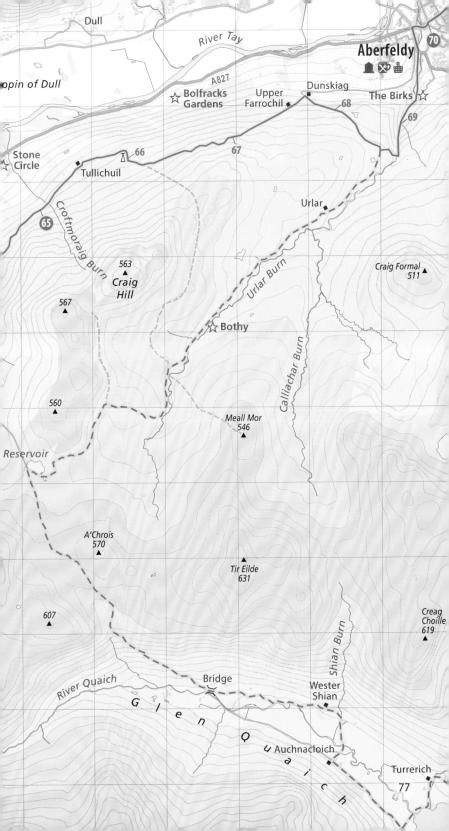

4 Reference

Origin of the Rob Roy Way

The Rob Roy Way was developed in 2001 and maintained over the years by an informal partnership between Rucksack Readers and the late John Henderson. John made a massive contribution to this route until his death in 2020 and he is sorely missed.

Our Inaugural Walk was held in May 2002, and the first edition of this guidebook was published soon afterwards. The next landmark was in 2011 when various grants enabled us to get the trail waymarked. In 2012 we gained recognition as one of *Scotland's Great Trails*: see
www.scotlandsgreattrails.com

Useful websites and contacts

Please refer to the official website before setting off. It was undergoing major overhaul in 2021, but from 2022 it will be updated regularly:
www.robroyway.com

Feedback on the route and this guidebook

If you have any issues with the route or with this guidebook, please email
info@rucsacs.com

Notes for novices

We provide notes on preparation, pace and choosing gear for those who lack experience of long-distance walking. Visit our home page
www.rucsacs.com
scroll to its foot and click *Notes for novices*.

NatureScot and SOAC

NatureScot is the government-funded body that works in partnership to care for Scotland's natural heritage:
www.nature.scot
It is also the custodian of Scotland's Great Trails, see:
www.scotlandsgreattrails.com
Details of the Scottish Outdoor Code are at
www.outdooraccess-scotland.scot

Forestry and Land Scotland (FLS)

FLS is responsible for managing, protecting and expanding Britain's forests and woodlands, with the aim of increasing their value to society and the environment:
forestryandland.gov.scot

Visitor information

VisitScotland is Scotland's tourist board and its website offers a wide range of useful information:
www.visitscotland.com
Its Visitor Information Centres are now called iCentres and you will find them in Aberfoyle and Pitlochry. For details, visit
www.rucsacs.com/rrw
and scroll down to view Route links. Callander has an informal information centre on its main street; its opening hours depend on the availability of volunteers.

Budget accommodation

For hostels in Callander and Pitlochry, visit
www.hostellingscotland.org.uk
For camping pods in Strathyre, visit
www.strathyrecampingpods.com
For B&B in Ardtalnaig, try Kindrochit (*jo@wildfoxevents.com*) or Holly Cottage (*info@loch-tay.net*).

Support services

A number of companies offer complete support packages for walking or cycling the Way, others such as Kingshouse Travel provide baggage and transfers. As of late 2021 we listed 16 such companies: visit
www.rucsacs.com/rrw and scroll down to view *Support Services*.

Transport

For journeys from anywhere to anywhere, try
www.rome2rio.com

Airlines and airports

British Airways *www.ba.com*
easyJet   *www.easyjet.com*
Edinburgh airport
www.edinburghairport.com
Glasgow airport
www.glasgowairport.com

Trains and buses

Traveline Scotland
www.travelinescotland.com
Citylink (buses)
www.citylink.co.uk
Train information:
www.scotrail.co.uk
www.thetrainline.com

Taxi

Aberfeldy Taxis 01887 820 370
Useful for travel around Aberfeldy including Amulree and Loch Tay generally. Book services well in advance. VisitScotland's website has a useful page about travel to/from Scotland with regulations for various countries and regions:
www.visitscotland.com/travel

Pronunciation guide

Place stress on the syllable shown in **bold**. Visitors to Scotland often find the soft, aspirated ch sound (as in 'loch') difficult to pronounce correctly. Try asking a native to demonstrate, then practise the sound: this may provide innocent amusement all round.

Ardeonaig	ar-**dron**-aig
Balquhidder	bal-**kwidd**-ur
Breachlaich	**braych**-lich
Breadalbane	bred-**awl**-ben
Culloden	cu-**lodd**-en
Drymen	**drimm**-en
Grandtully	**grant**-lee
Loch Katrine	Loch **Kat**-run
Quaich	kwaich
Schiehallion	shee-**hal**-yon
Stuc a Chroin	stooch-a-**chroyn**
Trossachs	**tross**-uchs
Venachar	**venn** ach-ar

Further reading

Of the books recommended below, the first is Scott's famous historical novel, the other two are biographies.

Scott, Walter (2008) *Rob Roy* OUP Oxford 560 pp 978-0-11-19954-988-5

Murray, W H (2000) *Rob Roy MacGregor* Canongate 314 pp 978-0-862415-38-9

Tranter, Nigel (2012) *Rob Roy MacGregor* Neil Wilson Publishing 3rd ed 192 pp 978-1-906000-18-9

Maps: online and printed

A detailed online route map is at
   www.rucsacs.com/rrw which you can zoom repeatedly for extreme detail.

Footprint Maps publish a *Rob Roy Way* folded sheet map at scale 1:40,000 on waterproof paper (revised in 2016). For more, see
   www.footprintmaps.co.uk.

For hill-walking and going off-route, more detailed maps are essential. Ordnance Survey's Explorers are larger scale at 1:25,000. Be sure to obtain the latest editions:
   www.ordnancesurvey.co.uk.

Saving Scotland's Red Squirrels

This fine website displays squirrel sightings on a map and asks you to report your sightings of both reds and greys:
   www.scottishsquirrels.org.uk

Midges and ticks

For midge facts and forecast, midge management and more, visit
   www.smidgeup.com

For practical advice about how to detect and remove ticks, and facts about Lyme disease, visit
   checkforticks.wordpress.com

Acknowledgements

The publisher is grateful to everybody who commented on this route and drafts of previous editions as well as this one. Above all, our thanks go to the late John Henderson, without whom the route would not exist in this form. He was a good friend and a great collaborator. We thank also Forestry and Land Scotland, the late Rennie McOwan, Perth & Kinross Countryside Trust, Scottish & Southern Energy plc, Stirling Council, Sustrans, Richard Sutton and Andy Wightman; and deepest thanks to Lindsay Merriman for her thorough proofreading at an exceptionally difficult time.

Photo credits

Barrie L Andrian/*www.crannog.co.uk* p21; Lindsay Anstett/Button Blog p46 (lower left); Andrew Curtis p69 (lower); Dewar's Aberfeldy p64 (lower); Forest Life Picture Library/ *www.forestry.gov.uk* p24 (upper), p26 (upper), p30 (lower left); John Henderson p44 (lower); Macs Adventure p5; *istockphoto.com*/topshotUK p24 (lower); David Morier/Royal Collection Trust p16; Paul Milligan p40 (upper), p51; Sandy Morrison p28 (upper), p29 (lower); Gordon Simm p26 (lower), p30 (lower right); VisitScotland Stirling p34 (lower), p40 (lower), p44 (upper), pp 54-55.

We thank also *Dreamstime.com* and photographers for the following images: Andrew Mitchell cover and p70 (lower); Lee Gillon title page; Uhg1234 p10; Sasalan999 pp14-15, p63 (middle); Chris148 p20 (lower); Mikelane45 p25 (upper); 12qwerty p25 (lower) and p27 (lower) ; Dbeatson p27 (upper); Leo6001 p29 (upper); Maxim Pyshnyy p30 (upper); Shawn Williams p43; Jeremy Brown p50 (upper); George Robertson p58 (upper), p63 (upper); Alistair Mcdonald p69 (upper); Tony Brindley p75; Douglas Mackenzie p73 (lower).

The remaining 70 photos are © Jacquetta Megarry.

Index